The Temple of Memories

The Temple of Memories

HISTORY, POWER,
AND MORALITY
IN A CHINESE VILLAGE

JUN JING

Stanford University Press
Stanford, California

Stanford University Press
Stanford, California

© 1996 by the Board of Trustees of the
Leland Stanford Junior University

Printed in the United States of America

CIP data appear at the end of the book

For my parents and Jeanne

Acknowledgments

My debt to James L. Watson is immeasurable. As my graduate advisor at Harvard University, Professor Watson first encouraged me to work in northwest China to investigate the problem of social memory. Professor Watson is a wonderful mentor and I owe him the deepest gratitude. I am also deeply grateful to Arthur Kleinman and K. C. Chang at Harvard. Professor Kleinman has been a constant intellectual stimulus. Professor Chang's unflinching sense of humor and optimism have raised my spirits on more than one occasion.

My intellectual journey at Harvard could not have been so enjoyable and rewarding an experience without the encouragement of other teachers, especially Thomas Barfield, Kenneth George, Michael Herzfeld, Roderick MacFarquhar, David Maybury-Lewis, Sally Moore, Pauline Peters, Parker Shipton, Stanley Tambiah, Rubie Watson, Nur Yalman, and Robin Yates. As conscientious educators and accomplished scholars, they offered a sympathetic ear and a guiding hand. They occupy a special place in my heart.

Many people offered invaluable suggestions after reading portions of the manuscript or listening to ideas in gestation. There is no way I can render unto them as much as I have received. A few who deserve particular mention are Helen Siu at Yale University, Robert Weller at Boston University, and Yan Yunxiang at the University of California, Los Angeles. And when the business of writing became too demanding, several friends extended logistical and emotional support. They include Sangmee Bak, Maris Gillette, Lida Junghans, Matthew Kohrman, Lu Qiwen, and Wang Daw-hwang.

Numerous funding and academic institutions provided "the iron rice bowl" that made this study possible. The Institute of Sociology at Beijing University gave me my first opportunity to work in northwest China during the summer of 1989. A Mellon Fellowship for Summer Research enabled me to travel from the United States to China's Gansu province in 1991. A semester of predissertation research in 1991 was supported by a Peabody Merit Scholarship. A 1992 Foreign Languages and Area Studies Fellowship supported my library research on Gansu and training in the local dialect. The National Science Foundation and the Wenner-Gren Foundation for Anthropological Research financed my fieldwork in 1992. The Beijing Social and Economic Survey Center served as the institutional sponsor for my fieldwork. My archival research in Taiwan in 1993 was aided by another Mellon Fellowship. The dissertation write-up was funded by a Charlotte W. Newcombe Doctoral Dissertation Fellowship of the Woodrow Wilson National Fellowship Foundation. I am grateful to all these organizations for their support.

At a critical point of revision, Myron Cohen at Columbia University carefully read the manuscript. His many insightful suggestions for improvement are immensely appreciated. I also owe a great debt of gratitude to Muriel Bell, my editor at Stanford University Press. Her enthusiastic support and editorial guidance carried me through the final stage of writing.

I convey special thanks to my parents, Jing Ruiyin and Li Yunpu, for having faith in my work. My deepest appreciation goes to my wife, Jeanne Moore, who has extended the boundaries of my compassion.

J. J.

Contents

Photographs follow p. 86

Maps

The Temple of Memories

1

Introduction: A Study of Social Memory

A Village Destroyed

The Kongs of Dachuan cannot forget that winter, more than three decades ago, when their village was effaced and life as they had known it ended. For much of 1960 they had ignored, then resisted, the government's declaration that their homes lay in the path of one of the more ambitious projects of the Great Leap Forward, and that by autumn's end they would have to make way for a hydroelectric dam and reservoir.[1]

But how could they, as Kongs who saw themselves as descendants of the ancient sage Confucius (*kong fu zi* in Chinese), abandon their ancestral tombs and the land that had been their haven for centuries? And, in any case, how, as one of them put it, could the mighty Yellow River really be "cut off at its waist"—a goal that had defeated the past efforts of Chinese and American engineers?[2]

So months lapsed, the deadline passed, and still the Kongs stayed on. And then, on a chill December night, the militia entered, shock troops of eviction, targeting first households without strong young men. Old women screamed and clung to their beds, refusing to leave. They were carried out bodily. The supporting pillars of their houses were roped to mules and pulled

down. As dawn broke, the frightened villagers began disman-
tling their own houses in a scramble to salvage what they could
to build shelter elsewhere. They hastily dug up the graves of immediate ancestors and close relatives, and, in violation of all tradition, unceremoniously threw bones in cement sacks or whatever other containers they could find for reburial on higher
ground. "It was no time for being proper about such things," an
elderly villager recalled years later. Nor did they have the physical strength to save older graves; the trauma of dislocation was
exacerbated by a debilitating famine, the worst in modern Chinese history.[3]

Under the double burden of hunger and shock, half the local
residents began resettling into other nearby communities while
the remaining population retreated a short distance uphill. In
March 1961, the Yellow River, China's second largest, was
stopped just downstream from Dachuan, its progress halted by
a dam 57 meters high. The river was compelled, by design, to
surge sideways to create a reservoir behind the dam. By the time
the dam's floodgate was lifted 48 hours later, much of Dachuan
was submerged, forever buried under the reservoir's waters.

The destruction of their village was the central event in a long
procession of tragedies for the Kongs under the new Communist
regime. Before 1949, the Kongs had dominated this part of northwest China's Gansu province. By status and name, they personi-
fied the old order that the Communist government had vowed
to supplant. Throughout the Maoist era (1949–76), the Kongs
were hit hard by assaults on the vestiges of old China, culminating, in their case, with the 1973–74 Campaign Against Lin Biao
and Confucius.[4] Only in the mid-1980's, with the gradual relax-
ation of political controls, did some of the Kongs consider it possible to reassert themselves and work toward some form of re-
dress and even healing.

My own path converged with that of the Kongs in the summer
of 1989, weeks after the military suppression of demonstrations
in Beijing's Tiananmen Square. At the time, I was a researcher
at Beijing University's Institute of Sociology, directed by the re-

nowned anthropologist Fei Xiaotong. Fei had earlier suggested as a research topic looking into the long-term consequences of population dislocation caused by water projects in northwest China. In fact, the institute's initial findings had already figured in the debate over building a dam at the Yangtze River's Three Gorges. With the university effectively shut down, first by the student protests and then by the political crackdown, and with little interest in remaining in Beijing, where friends and colleagues were being arrested, several of us decided to resume that research. Thus, in July 1989 I set off with another researcher and two graduate students for Gansu and my first encounter with the Kongs in the relocated village of Dachuan. At first, I expected this to be a short-term study, mostly about reservoir resettlement. Instead, I returned to Dachuan, after entering the doctoral program in anthropology at Harvard University, to spend the summer of 1991, eight months in 1992, and brief stays in 1993 and 1995, learning not only about resettlement, but about other aspects of the local experience of radical socialism during the Maoist era and about the terms of life in the post-Mao period.

The 1989 trip was to prove to be my first field research into the range of issues generally addressed by scholars under the heading "social memory." The ultimate goal of social memory research is to investigate the transformative impact of group-life requirements and collective interests upon the overall framework and specific contents of personal recollections. As explained below, Dachuan is an ideal place for this kind of research.

The Regional Setting of Fieldwork

The village of Dachuan is about 80 kilometers southwest of Lanzhou, Gansu's provincial capital. On the map of China, Gansu is a long, diagonal wedge, bounded by Shaanxi on the east, Sichuan on the south, Xinjiang on the west, the Qinghai-Tibet highlands on the southwest, and Ningxia and Inner Mongolia on the north. In other words, Gansu forms the narrow corridor

1. Location of Gansu province in the People's Republic of China.

linking China's heartland to Inner Asia, a vast terrain settled by Tibetans, Mongolians, Uighurs, Chinese-speaking Muslims, and many other ethnic groups. For centuries, China's attempts to control its northwest frontiers have relied on the passageway provided by Gansu.

Given its strategic importance, it is not surprising that the province's capital originated as a military outpost in 86 B.C. When this outpost became, in A.D. 581, the seat of a prefectural government (Wei 1988: 9), it was named Lanzhou, or "Mount Lan Prefecture." Mount Lan is actually a range of loess hills south of the once-walled city. Hemmed in by these hills on one side and the Yellow River on the other, the city has by now grown into an hourglass-shaped metropolis. Its commercial center in the north and its industrial district in the south are linked by a road about ten kilometers long.

Lanzhou was a major center of caravan traffic until World War

II. It has since been linked by rail to Xinjiang, Qinghai, and Inner Mongolia. It is also connected by rail to an important depot in Qinghai, which serves as the staging point for trucks and buses headed for Lhasa. In 1948, the city had 160,000 residents (China Handbook Editorial Board 1950: 43). The population now exceeds two million.

Rapid industrialization since the Communist takeover in 1949 has turned Lanzhou into northwest China's second-largest industrial center, after Xian. From the start, its industrial programs emphasized the province's mineral resources and, consequently, heavy industry. This emphasis also set the pattern for the industrialization of the province's smaller cities. Rich deposits of coal and iron ore provided the base of Gansu's ferrous metal industry, which produces pig iron, steel, steel alloys, and ferrosilicon. Abundant copper, nickel, lead, and zinc deposits supplied its nonferrous metal industry (World Bank 1988: 40). These heavy industry projects have benefited from the construction of large-scale dams and electric-generating plants on the upper reaches of the Yellow River.

Over 65 percent of Gansu's 20 million people lived in rural areas in 1992. Its rural population had, in 1984, the lowest per capita income in China—221 yuan, compared with a national average of 356 yuan (World Bank 1988: 1). In the early 1990's, its rural population remained the nation's poorest (State Statistics Bureau 1992, 1993a). This persistence of poverty owes much to Gansu's natural environment: a short growing season, sparse rainfall, and severe soil erosion.

Social conditions also have contributed to poverty. In the first half of the twentieth century, Gansu was plagued by official corruption, relentless military conscription, ethnic tensions, and almost constant warfare (see Ekvall 1938: 64–69; Lipman 1980, 1984: 285–316, 1990: 65–86; Perry 1983: 355–82). Under the collective farming system, from 1958 to 1981, deforestation, population resettlement, aggressive efforts to expand farmland, and major hydroelectric projects combined to aggravate Gansu's ecological depredation (Greer 1979; Jing 1989; Smil 1984: 10–61;

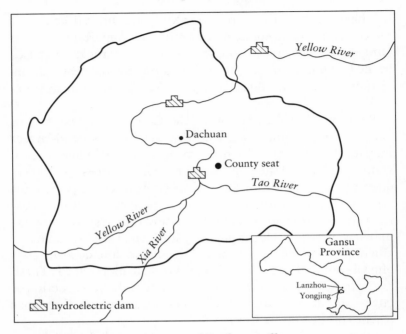

2. *Lanzhou, Yongjing county, and Dachuan village.*

Wang 1989). Since the mid-1980's, this province has been a major recipient of special poverty-relief loans from the central government.

Basic Information About Dachuan Village

Dachuan, which means "big valley," is under the jurisdiction of a rural county named Yongjing. The village is perched at the midpoint of an S-shaped valley carved by the Yellow River as it cascades down from the Qinghai-Tibet plateau. Its residential area is clustered on the slope between the reservoir built in 1961 and a barren mountain range. A 1992 village census recorded 3,310 residents and 638 locally registered households. Most of Dachuan's residents depend on farming for their basic livelihood; their chief crops are wheat, maize, and potatoes. However, reservoir construction and population growth have reduced the village's per capita farmland to 0.6 *mu* (one *mu* is about one-sixth of an acre). This extremely limited amount of farmland has made it virtually impossible for villagers to meet their basic needs solely through agriculture.

Dachuan is nonetheless better off than many nearby communities, thanks to the villagers' persistent search for seasonal jobs in cities and at state-run construction sites. And from the early 1980's to 1992, local people dug more than 100 fish ponds from the salty marshes on the edge of the reservoir. These fish ponds, along with the outside jobs, are important sources of cash income. Even so, the village is mired in extreme poverty. When I revisited Dachuan in September 1993, its chief administrator calculated that nearly 40 percent of the local households were still living below the official poverty line, set in Yongjing at an annual per capita income of 300–400 yuan, or $50–$65 by the official exchange rates that year.

In its outward appearance, Dachuan resembles many other villages in this part of Gansu. The typical dwelling is set within a walled courtyard. The central hall invariably faces south, flanked by perpendicular side rooms facing east and west. The buildings are mostly made of rammed earth walls and wooden pillars, which support roofs that are generally tilted slightly downward toward the courtyard. In contrast to the barren and windswept mountains behind the village and across the river, the settlement is encircled by thickets of poplars planted along dirt paths and between fields. Apple and pear trees are grown within walled courtyards and enclosed gardens. Reforestation has been a major achievement in Dachuan since the termination of the collective farming system in 1981. The village boasted 200 mature trees per household in 1992, all privately owned.

Local Kinship Structure

Interpersonal relations in Dachuan are tightly knit by descent and marriage. Although it is not a single-surname village, 85 percent of the local households in 1992 were surnamed Kong. The balance comprised 16 other surnames. Except for a group surnamed Li, whose ancestors had settled in Dachuan earlier than the Kongs, the others came to the village as refugees from war and famine in the late nineteenth century and during the first quarter of the twentieth century. In 1992, over 25 percent of the married women in the other surname groups were Kongs.

Dachuan also has been the center of a large ancestral cult, whose members, roughly 20,000 people in 1992, are surnamed Kong and are distributed over 23 villages within Yongjing county. These Kongs trace their ancestry to Confucius through a Guangdong-born ancestor who migrated to Gansu and settled in Lanzhou about six centuries ago. He is said to have been related to the Guangdong branch (*ling nan pai*) of the nationwide Kong clan headquartered in Confucius's hometown of Qufu, in the coastal province of Shandong. The genealogical claim of the Kongs in Yongjing was not formally recognized by the Qufu-based council of clan elders until 1937, when the *Confucius Clan Genealogy (kong zi shi jia pu)* was updated and expanded to include not only the Kongs in Qufu but also those scattered throughout China.[5] Despite the rather late recognition by Qufu, the Kongs in Dachuan and adjacent Kong villages had long identified themselves with the Confucian heritage by three means: a carefully guarded collection of genealogical records, a cycle of ancestral rituals, and a temple dedicated to Confucius.

It was around the year 1500 that a group of Kongs originally living in a village near Lanzhou moved to Dachuan. Since the four men heading this group were brothers and were buried in the village after death, the Kongs of Yongjing consider Dachuan their "old settlement" (*lao zhuang*). From a historical point of view, the social organization of the Kongs in Yongjing constituted what historians and anthropologists specializing in China call "a higher-order lineage" (see H. Baker 1979: 67–70; Freedman 1966: 19–21, J. Watson 1982b: 608–9). The nucleus of this lineage was Dachuan's Confucius temple—a corporate estate and a fixed site at which its members could celebrate ritual unity. The institutional framework of this multivillage lineage broke down under the blows of Maoist campaigns, but, as we shall see, its recovery was evident by the mid-1980's.

Because they trace local history to the four brothers who settled and then died in Dachuan, the Kongs in the valley of Yongjing county have been divided into four sublineages locally known as the "four gates" (si men). Population growth, economic pressures, and reservoir construction have forced many Kongs to leave Dachuan for other places. However, members of all four sublineages are still found in the relocated village of Dachuan, whereas the Kongs in the other 22 Yongjing villages tend to be from just one or two of the four sublineages that originated in Dachuan.

Village Administration

The Kongs living in Dachuan itself have been further divided into eight smaller divisions. This eight-part structure of agnatic kinship evidently influenced the local implementation of the collective farming system known as "people's communes." In force throughout rural China from 1958 to the early 1980's, this system had three institutional components. At the lowest level was the "production team." Its leaders were responsible not only for daily job assignments to team members, but for distributing "work points" (gong fen), which were in effect cash or material rewards calculated on the basis of work performance, taking into account team members' sex, age, health, skills, and education. At the middle level was the "production brigade," whose leaders drew up the general agricultural production plan to be implemented by the production teams. Usually, a production brigade comprised several production teams within a village, making brigade leaders a village's most influential cadres. At the top level was the "commune," the administrators of which were appointed by county-level authorities. The administrative body and the Communist Party committee of a given "commune" were in charge of the selection of village-level cadres.

The way a "production brigade" was formed in Dachuan was

apparently influenced by what anthropologists call "the social distance of kinship" (see Sahlins 1972: 189–204), a principle of political loyalty and economic reciprocity based on differentiated ties between kin. As mentioned above, the Kongs divided themselves into four sublineages, which in Dachuan became eight smaller divisions. In the past, the eight divisions were reflected in clearly demarcated residential areas within Dachuan. They also had separate territories for orchards, farm fields, threshing grounds, and graveyards. When a "production brigade" was organized in Dachuan, the eight Kong divisions within the village formed themselves into eight "production teams" and retained their separate territories. After the village was relocated in 1961 to higher ground in the vicinity, farming and residential territories were re-established, primarily along kinship boundaries.

In 1981, the commune system was ended at Dachuan in favor of agricultural work by individual households. The name "production teams" was changed to "economic cooperatives," which in Dachuan have maintained identifiable boundaries of residential and farming areas, boundaries drawn on the basis of the eightfold divisions of the Kong lineage. Each "economic cooperative" therefore represents a social microcosm within the village's overall structures of residence, administration, property relations, public security, personal ties, and marriages between Kongs and others.

Within the agnatic kinship of the Kongs, close relatives trace ancestry through five generations to a common ancestor instead of going all the way back to the four brothers who first settled in Dachuan. This type of agnatic relation is known as the "five mourning grades" (*wu fu*), a popular reference in Chinese culture to the five kinds of attires required of agnates at funerals (see Wolf 1970: 189–207). In the eyes of Dachuan's residents, all Kongs living in this village and elsewhere in Yongjing are relatives, but only those within the five mourning grades are primary agnates. In theory, these agnates are under the greatest obligation to participate in one another's life-cycle rituals, especially funerals; they are also expected to provide mutual assistance in times of crisis.

The Kongs have long dominated Dachuan both in numbers and in public positions. From 1950 to 1992, the village chief, the local Party boss, the accountant-general, the production team leaders, and the local primary school's principal were all surnamed Kong. It was only in 1993 that a Mr. Luo was appointed by higher authorities to take charge of the village's primary school.

As in other parts of rural China, Dachuan's local administrators are called "village cadres" (cun gan bu). The administrative power of Dachuan's cadres has declined markedly since the village was decollectivized. But still, they wield a great degree of control when it comes to collecting agricultural taxes, organizing labor for public works, redrawing land allocations to cope with population changes, and implementing the government's birth control policy. In terms of personal wealth and opportunities to take advantage of the entrepreneurial thrust of post-Mao economic reforms, the cadres and former cadres of Dachuan have an unbeatable edge in business situations that require networks of connections, bank loans, travel experience, market information, legal knowledge, and inside word on state policies.[6]

A Social History of Remembering

Although my fieldwork touched on many historical and contemporary aspects of village life in Dachuan, the ethnographic data analyzed throughout this book focus on the rebuilding of a local temple for the worship of Confucius and local Kong ancestors. It will be explained in Chapter 2 why I call this site a "Confucius temple" instead of an "ancestral hall." Rebuilt in 1991, this temple played a pivotal role in the reconstruction of Dachuan's religious life, kinship ideology, and power structure. All specific isues related to this temple will be examined from the theoretical perspective of social memory. These include ritual knowledge, the writing of genealogies, popular images of village history, narratives of suffering, the politics of revenge, conflicting perceptions of rituals' significance, and attitudes towards China's experiments with radical socialism. By examining how memories are articulated and transmitted through activities centered around Dachuan's Confucius temple, this study offers a bottom-up approach to the problem of remembrance in a country where mass amnesia and selective remembrance have been vigorously promoted by state authorities.

At first glance, the story of Dachuan's Confucius temple may suggest that many traditional ideas and practices prohibited under the first decades of Communist rule have been revived. But a closer look reveals a far more complicated picture. These ideas and practices are not mechanically retrieved from the past; they are blended with cultural inventions, shaped by the local experience of Maoism, and permeated with contemporary concerns. As a landmark of local history, the rebuilt Confucius temple certainly evokes a wide range of memories of this village's pre-Communist past, when the Kongs enjoyed a prestige that owed much to their identification with Confucius and their previous political influence and economic status. It is important to bear in mind, however, that the rebuilding of this temple had everything to do with the Kongs' efforts to make sense of their troubled experience under Mao Zedong's rule and the social changes of the post-Mao era. It is thus best to regard the story of Dachuan's Confucius temple, to borrow a phrase from Peter Burke, as "a social history of remembering" (1989: 100).

The Dachuan material furnishes an especially interesting basis for formulating cross-cultural comparisons. In a study of how men and women remembered their work lives in an American automobile plant from World War II to 1961, John Bodnar (1989: 1201–21) noticed several consistent themes in the autobiographical narratives of these retired workers. Commenting on such themes, he pointed out: "Memory was a cognitive device by which historical actors sought to interpret the reality they had lived—and, it appears, they could never do so alone, without reference to a social context" (1989: 1202). One might ask: What is this "social context" that narrators of history must invoke? This seemingly simple question has been in fact at the very heart of social memory research from its inception.

The Social Basis of Memory

Psychologists began studying memory a century ago, but, with some exceptions, their research was conducted in laboratory settings, using formal experimental techniques to answer theoretical questions about the general principles that govern the workings of memory. In an attempt to endow psychology with scientific respectability, the experimental methods invented by Hermann Ebbinghaus ([1885] 1964) to test the results of verbal learning were embraced and developed. In typical experiments on memory, stimuli such as nonsense syllables were used as the objects for recall. The human subjects were carefully selected and instructed. The experimental environment was standardized and the amount of time the subjects needed to recall stimuli was painstakingly recorded.

These experiments tended to ignore the complex workings of memory in real-life contexts, and they generated few insights into the social basis of remembrance. At a 1976 conference attended mainly by English-speaking psychologists to discuss the practical aspects of memory, Ulric Neisser characterized the inadequacies of research on the social origin of memory by a simple formula: "If X is an interesting or socially significant aspect of memory, then psychologists have hardly ever studied X" (1978: 4). This was a fairly accurate criticism of the state of memory research in psychology up to the late 1970's.

The same criticism could have been applied to sociology and anthropology were it not for the valuable work by the French scholar Maurice Halbwachs (1877–1945), a disciple and younger colleague of Emile Durkheim. It was in 1925 that Halbwachs developed the concept of "collective memory" and applied it to his studies of how the past is remembered within the milieux of families, religious groups, and social classes. Rejecting various psychological interpretations of memory then gaining currency in Europe, he argued that any discussion of the origin of personal recollections must take into account the impact of such social institutions as kinship, community, religion, political organization, social class, and nation. As an illustration of his central argument, he contended that in stable community life every family has its privately cherished memories and secrets, revealed to none but its own members. This "family memory" (*mémoire familiale*) is not merely a collage of individual recollections. Rather, it is a collective reworking of the past (Halbwachs [1925] 1952: 287).

There is little doubt that Halbwachs was faithful to the fundamentals of Durkheimian sociology, but he was not a blind follower. That he was an imaginative thinker becomes apparent when one looks at what he added to Durkheim's insights. For example, after developing the concept of "mechanical" and "organic" solidarity in *The Division of Labor in Society* ([1930] 1964), Durkheim focused on the idea of "collective consciousness"—that is, "the body of beliefs and sentiments common to the average of the members of a society" (Aron 1970: 15). For Durkheim, collective consciousness embraces the greater part of individual existence rather than the desire of any particular persons (Aron 1970: 11–24). As he saw it, the prospect of purely individual thought is almost an absurdity, since language and conceptualization develop through social interaction. Phrased differently, the source of collective identity, morality, and religion, in Durkheim's view, is the individual's experience of society, a force greater than oneself and requiring one's allegiance (Douglas 1980: 8).

Proceeding from this argument, Durkheim was able to develop the concept of "collective effervescence" and to interpret it as the foundation of human cultural creativity in the spheres of tribal ceremonies, ritual dances, festival meals, or public holidays. In many pages devoted to this concept, he attempted to demonstrate that cultural creativity is largely rooted in collective enthusiasm, shared sentiments, and unified interests, quite contrary to the then fashionable thought that cultural creativity is the privilege of a handful of individuals.

Yet there is a problem with Durkheim's thinking. Even if we assume that societies or groups exhibit cultural creativity and renewal through the celebration of ritual unity in periods of effervescence, one must ask what binds people together in periods of calm, when routine behavior is the order of the day. This problem was successfully addressed by Halbwachs, who argued that it is collective memory that keeps the recall of past events alive in everyday life, making the ritualized re-enactments of history and the excited celebrations of group identity possible over time (see Coser 1992 for a fuller discussion).

In retrospect, Halbwachs developed quite original ideas on the issue of memory, best illustrated in three of his works. The first is *Les Cadres sociaux de la mémoire* ([1925] 1952), which lays out his basic theory of collective memory. The second is *La Topographie légendaire des évangiles en terre sainte: Etude de mémoire collective* (1941), a historical study of how Christians, including the Crusaders, employed memories of their religious upbringing to discover, sometimes with great imagination, holy sites during their visits to Jerusalem. The third is *La Mémoire collective* ([1950] 1980), an application of his theory to the analysis of childhood memories, perceptions of time and space, and differences between history and memory.[7]

Three Approaches in Social Memory Research

The trailblazing research by Halbwachs did not attract much attention outside France until the 1970's, when it was taken up by historians and social scientists attempting to move beyond the purely psychological discussion of memory. Among recent studies of social memory, at least three basic approaches can be discerned.

THE COLLECTIVE MEMORY APPROACH

Following Halbwachs, social historians, anthropologists, and sociologists have tried to investigate what members of a social group share of their past and how (see, e.g., Rosaldo 1980; Schuman & Scott 1989:359–81; Schwartz 1991:221–36; Valensi 1986:283–305). To this end, Paul Connerton (1989) has explored the importance of ritualized re-enactments of myth and history, while Françoise Zonabend (1985) has examined notions of local history in a French village characterized by an intricate web of relationships connecting family, church, school, and work place.

THE OFFICIAL MEMORY APPROACH

This is an attempt to scrutinize how public notions of history are manipulated by dominant sectors of society through mass media, the education system, mainstream art, public commemorations, and committees of official chronologists (see, e.g., K. Baker 1990; Goody 1986, 1987; Kuper 1983: 33–54; Lindstrom 1982: 316–29). In this connection, Lynn Hunt (1984), Hobsbawm and associates (1984), and Chritel Lane (1981) have concentrated on the manipulation of society's memory by different political regimes in the area of calendar reforms, court rituals, historical celebrations, and national holidays.

THE POPULAR MEMORY APPROACH

Scholars interested in the issue of popular resistance have tried to come to grips with the elusive and often semi-secret views of history shared by members of certain social segments who do not necessarily adhere to the dominant, public, or official representations of the past (see, especially, Popular Memory Group 1982; R. Watson 1994). The articulation of countermemories is analyzed as evidence of resistance against various forms of domination. A relevant case is James Scott's study of a Malaysian village in which, he argues, the negative impact of mechanized farming was condemned by impoverished villagers through the creation of "a remembered economy" that glossed over many unattractive features of an older system of land tenure (Scott 1985: 178–83). The relationship between memory and resistance has been a particularly constant theme in anthropological studies of ethnicity (see Handler and Linnekin 1984: 273–90; Hanson 1989: 890–902; Herzfeld 1985, 1986; Rappaport 1990). Provoked in critical moments of contact with the outside world, the workings of ethnic memory provide a basis for the assertion of identity, serving to mobilize ethnic groups vis-à-vis dominant cultures and the social changes confronting them.

From Memory Research to China Studies

Research on social memory in China involves particular challenges. Chinese culture claims unusual continuity over several thousand years and many thousands of miles. "This continuity and unity are found most markedly in the philosophy, political theory, and ethics that are subsumed under the tradition of Confucian thought and in the Buddhist and Taoist impacts on art, poetry, and religion" (Diamond 1969: 1). A key factor in China's cultural continuity is a complex system of knowledge transmission. A worthy Chinese is supposed not only to remember a vast amount of information related to the past, but to draw on this past as a basis of moral reasoning (Elvin 1991: 33–61; Ryckmans 1986; Schwarcz 1991: 85–109).

In imperial China, memorizing essential texts was absolutely crucial for those who hoped to rise through the civil service examinations (Chaffee 1985; Miyazaki 1976; Lee 1985). This practice remains important in contemporary China, especially for ambitious urban youth trying to succeed in a highly competitive education system (see Gardner 1989; Shirk 1982). Starting in primary school, children begin memorizing the dates of ancient dynasties, names of historic figures, and lengthy passages from classical poems.

The meticulous remembrance of past events and persons is equally important for those living in rural areas, where local history is entwined with the identities of descent-based groups. The outlook and behavior of those who grow up within these groups are indelibly molded by a process of learning about their past through a multitude of oral, written, and performative media. A well-known case is ancestor worship, "the essential religion of the Chinese" (C. K. Yang 1961: 53). Relying on lineage rhetoric, sacrificial rites, and the updating of genealogies, it evokes memories of the dead to remind each generation of its identity and obligations (see, e.g., R. Watson 1988: 203–27). Other public acts of remembrance such as boat races, temple festivities, and local theater also constitute a highly emotional display of group identities in the countryside, where more than 80 percent of the Chinese people live.

A special difficulty in studying social memory in contemporary China arises from the attempts of Maoist social engineers to dictate remembrance and forgetting (Dirlik 1978; Feuerwerker 1968; Madsen 1990: 149–74; Schwarcz 1987: 177–79). Even today, Chinese authorities seek tight control over society's memory at several levels. At the archival level, such control takes the form of restricting access to historical documents. At the level of mass media and public education, control is exercised through censorship, political propaganda, and the careful writing and rewriting of history textbooks. At a more personal level, control relies on intimidation and, sometimes, physical punishment of those who offer a radically different and unwelcome version of the past, particularly when it touches on the history of the Communist Party. These forms of political control of society's memory have been researched mainly in terms of the relations between the state and intellectuals (see Goldman 1967; Goldman, Cheek, & Mamrin 1983; Unger 1993). But much more work has to be done, especially bottom-up studies that focus on local reactions to the official manipulations of social memory.

There is also an urgent need to link social memory studies with more general research on the impact of Maoist campaigns and post-Mao economic reforms. We are reminded by Gregory Ruf's study (1994) of rural life in Sichuan province that the emergence of a market economy has presented new opportunities for some of the village and township administrators who are able to adjust to the post-Mao reforms successfully. Since the end of the collective farming system, says Ruf, many local cadres have seen their power erode until, reduced to virtual figurehead status, they are no longer able to collect taxes, to mediate disputes, or to discharge effectively the administrative responsibilities entrusted to them by the state. Others, in contrast, have constructed new bases for their political legitimacy, promoting themselves among local constituents as successful entrepreneurs with useful ties to higher officials or commercial enterprises. Moreover, many rural residents and townspeople from outside the party-state bureaucracy have risen to prominence by deftly portraying themselves as representatives of local community interests.

Yan Yunxiang (1992) has outlined a more dramatic cycle of reversed fortunes in the course of political upheavals and post-Mao reforms. In the early 1950's, Yan points out, many poor villagers became political activists during the Communist drives for land reform and thus gained dominance over those who were designated as members of the "exploiting class," usually landowners. Some of these political activists became village cadres, only to be replaced later, sometimes in humiliating fashion, by better-educated people or more aggressive contenders for power. With the introduction of economic reforms in the early 1980's, it was not rare to find former village cadres sliding down the social ladder (Yan 1992: 3–20). Meanwhile, some of the people who had been stigmatized as members of the exploiting class quickly regained a measure of prosperity and even political influence. Given that these reversals took place in a relatively short time, it would be reasonable to expect memories of Maoism to be contradictory and possibly threatening if articulated in a local community.

In fact, a number of recent ethnographies have offered convincing evidence that memories of Maoist socialism forcefully affect the current behavior and political attitudes of Chinese citizens (Huang 1989; Kleinman 1986; Potter & Potter 1990: 255–56; Siu 1989a; 1989b: 195–212; 1990: 765–94; R. Watson 1994; Yan 1992; M. Yang 1986, 1989). These studies show that exposure to new ideas, broader social contacts, and value shifts that have occurred since the 1980's tend to reshape memories of the Maoist era, informing them with fresh meanings and new terms of reference.

Two Themes of This Book

Fascinated by various elements of the social memory research outlined above, I resumed my study of Dachuan in 1992 to ask questions, listen, and try to understand how the village's past animated the lives of its residents. The result is an account of the workings of memory in a rural community that has made grand claims on history and undergone drastic changes since the Communist victory. In the following chapters, the Dachuan data will be examined under two major themes. The first concerns human suffering, including individual misfortunes and communal defeats. The second involves attempts to cope with suffering and to recover from political persecution, economic deprivation, and cultural disruption.

The importance of exploring the first theme lies in the fact that many residents of Dachuan were badly victimized from the early 1950's to the mid-1970's. In this period, more than 150 people, either surnamed Kong or related to the Kongs by marriage, lived as outcasts because they or their parents were identified in political campaigns as "class enemies," "bad elements," "counterrevolutionaries," "rich peasants," "big landlords," or "practitioners of feudal superstition." As described earlier, the construction of the reservoir caused the destruction of the village, the dispersal of its people, and the loss of much farmland and hundreds of family tombs. Coinciding with resettlement were the disastrous man-made shortages of food and medicine during the Great Leap Forward of 1958–61, which contributed to at least 50 deaths in Dachuan. In one extreme but not unique example of the cultural disruption precipitated by political campaigns, the Kongs had to undergo the humiliation of attending public rallies called to denounce their famous ancestor during a national anti-Confucius drive launched in 1974 by Mao Zedong.

The sufferings of the Kongs during the Maoist era were mirrored in the troubled fate of the village's Confucius temple. Its ritual land was confiscated in the early 1950's by government officials promoting land reform. Then, the educated elites in charge of the temple's ritual land, ceremonial services, and primary school were targeted for political persecution, including physical abuse and public humiliation. All temple activities ceased. At the onset of the Great Leap Forward, the temple was first sealed off by a government decree and then damaged by the reservoir. Finally, just as the Maoist era was drawing to a close, the temple's damaged and closed buildings were torn down.

The need to examine the second theme of Dachuan's history derives from a later recovery phase, made possible by the Chinese leadership's adoption in the early 1980's of rural reforms that replaced the radical Maoist model of national development. Paralleling Dachuan's recovery was a progression of events culminating in the reconstruction of the Confucius temple. While it honors the distant past of an illustrious descent line, this sacred site also serves as a monument to the recent history of a severely wounded community. It represents a hard-won opportunity to resume the transmission of religious values and ritual knowledge.

In social and political terms, the reappearance of the Dachuan temple epitomizes a radical reversal of power relations. The reconstruction project was led by a group of middle-aged and elderly male villagers, all of whom were surnamed Kong and most of whom had suffered political persecution and social discrimination under Mao's rule.

Their rise to prominence in the 1980's was made possible by the assertive roles they came to play in two important areas of village life. The elderly members of this group provided badly needed ritual expertise after a provisional ancestor shrine was first set up in 1984. They then worked together to prepare for the rebuilding of the Confucius temple. The younger members of this group were, from the mid-1980's onward, activists in a local movement to secure compensation from state agencies for the reservoir-caused resettlement. They eventually became the top cadres of Dachuan and joined forces with the elderly ritual experts to raise money to rebuild the Confucius temple. The alliance of these people for the temple's reconstruction suggests a transformation of the local-level social order and power relations. The story of Dachuan and its Confucius temple, in short, is one of a proud and innovative people trying to rebuild their lives after grievous assaults on their cultural identity, sense of history, and religious faith.

2

Memory of Historical Possibilities

Entering the Temple

From the Yongjing county seat, a six-kilometer paved road leads to a dirt path running through the relocated village of Dachuan. At the intersection of this path and a residential lane is an enclosure of high mud-brick walls with, on its southern side, an imposing gate with cast-iron handles. Once inside this gate, a towering wooden structure can be seen. The vertical plaque over its entrance signals that this is *da cheng dian*—the Monumental Hall of Great Accomplishment. Its beams, eaves, columns, and bracketings are clear-varnished, rather than painted as is often the case in Chinese temples, giving the building a wonderful golden glow. To its sides are classrooms for preschoolers and a watchman's office-cum-bedroom.

The reader will want to know why this sacred site is identified in this study as a "Confucius temple," and why its central building is called by the local people "Monumental Hall of Great Accomplishment." The Chinese term for "temple" is *si* in the Buddhist tradition and *guan* in the Taoist tradition. Neither is ordinarily applied to the buildings erected in memory of great men and ancestors, which usually are called *ci* and *ci tang*, respectively. In Chinese popular religion, the temples enshrining medicine gods, fertility goddesses, flood-control deities, and other supernatural beings are often named *miao*. Interestingly, the architectural complexes once found across China for the worship of Confucius and prominent Confucian scholars also were frequently called *miao*. During the Tang dynasty (618–906 A.D.), for instance, these structures were called *xian sheng miao* or "Ancient Saint Temples." The two most popular terms that lasted into the twentieth century were *wen miao*, literally "Temples of Literature," and *kong zi miao*, sometimes simply *kong miao*, which should be translated as "Confucius Temple" or "Temple of Master Kong." In all existing Confucius temples, the central halls are known as *da cheng dian*, that is, "Monumental Halls of Great Accomplishment." The largest central hall and the largest temple complex ever built for the worship of Confucius are in Qufu, the ancient sage's birth and burial place.

Turning back to the Confucius temple in Dachuan, the earliest documented reference to its historical existence is a register of sheep sacrificed from 1643 to 1664. This document appears in a ten-volume genealogy, compiled in 1905 on the basis of even older lineage documents. Judging from this handwritten genealogy (Kong Xianmin 1905) and other historical documents kept by the Kongs and at Yongjing county's archives, the temple was renovated in 1756, destroyed in 1785, and rebuilt in 1792. It was looted and burned in 1864, when the village was raided by Muslim insurgents from a nearby market town. The temple was not restored until 1934. The causes of its destruction before the nineteenth century are not known; its destruction in 1864 can be verified by written documents and orally transmitted accounts.

A Landmark of Ethnic Conflict

During the reign of the Tongzhi Emperor (1862–74), a wave of Muslim rebellions swept northwest China. Devastating battles were waged in Gansu for thirteen years between the Han Chinese and the followers of Islam. Fields went unplanted; massive bloodshed was frequent. The population of Gansu, which then included what are now Qinghai and Ningxia, plummeted from fifteen million to three million, according to one Christian missionary source (Ekvall 1938:23). Chinese demographers estimate that Gansu's population dropped from 14.7 million in 1862 to 4.6 million in 1874, and that the most disastrous year was 1870, when two million people perished (Zhao Wenlin & Xie Shujun 1988:414–15). By the time the Muslim rebellions were put down by Zuo Zongtang, the governor-general of Gansu and Shaanxi provinces, Gansu had become a land of deserted villages and untilled fields (Fields 1978; Lipman 1980).

Dachuan was devastated in this storm of ethnic violence. Not far away was the market town of Hezhou, now called Linxia and known as China's "little Mecca" (Gladney 1991:47–58), the stronghold of Ma Haiyan, Ma Zhan'ao, and Ma Qianling—three of the best-known Muslim rebel leaders in the northwest. Before surrendering to Zuo Zongtang, they fought fierce battles with government troops and Han Chinese militiamen. In an area now under the administration of Yongjing, Lingtao, and Dongxiang counties, Han Chinese villagers formed a military confederation under the command of three Kongs, two of whom were from Dachuan.

Casualties on both sides were enormous. A "county gazetteer," a historical record compiled by local officials, attests that more than 1,000 Chinese militiamen were killed in 1864 alone. Of these casualties, 130 were reported to be from Dachuan (Zhang Guochang [1892] 1917, vol. 12). In the same year, an even greater number of women and children met their death when the rammed-earth walls of the villages in the Dachuan area were brought down by Muslim soldiers. More than 600 women and children related to the Kongs by birth or marriage were slain outright, burned to death, or committed suicide (Zhang Guochang [1892] 1917, vol. 13, pp. 26–31). Dachuan's Confucius temple was burned down.

The irony is that the destruction of Dachuan and its Confucius temple had its roots in a local marriage, an aspect of a secret history that my older informants did not at first want to discuss.

According to oral accounts I eventually managed to collect and piece together, a Muslim woman from a village across the river had married into Dachuan, to a member of the fourth segment of the Kong lineage. This marriage obviously took place well before ethnic tensions erupted in large-scale warfare in the Dachuan area.

Jonathan Lipman, a specialist in Muslim issues in northwest China, postulates that the Han-Muslim conflicts, which began emerging in the late eighteenth century and then exploded again during the second half of the nineteenth century, coincided with the introduction and expansion of Central Asian Sufism into China. At the onset, "the Sufis who came to China made each other the immediate objects of violence, rather than the state or the Hans," says Lipman, adding that competing Sufi orders "fought over mosque-building rights, over territory, over loyalty to different *shaykhs* (saints), over matters of ritual" (Lipman 1990: 69). In addition, the Sufi orders also engaged in violent disputes with the traditional orders of Islam in China, known by the generic term of *lao jiao* ("the old doctrine") and with local Han Chinese communities. The mishandling of such disputes and the often harsh punishment against Muslim leaders by Han officials triggered confrontations between local bureaucrats and Muslim communities, which in turn exacerbated existing conflicts between Muslim and Han communities.

By the second half of the nineteenth century, the offspring of the aforementioned Kong-Muslim marriage in Dachuan numbered around 300, according to several village elders who had learned from their parents and grandparents about the bloodshed of 1864. In interviews, they referred to the descendants of the Kong-Muslim marriage as Kong Huihui, Huihui being the local term for the Hui people, who are Chinese-speaking Muslims. It is said that the descendants of this mixed marriage were converted to Islam by their Muslim relatives. They were allowed to have their own separate residential quarter, a prayer hall, and an Islamic-style cemetery in the vicinity of Dachuan. The original site of that cemetery is now a farm field, but the people of Dachuan still call it *hui hui tai*, "Huihui Mound."

The decisive factor in Dachuan's devastation in 1864 was the leading role of Kongs in the confederation of Han militias who sided with the government troops. For the Muslim rebel leaders in Hezhou, destroying Dachuan would eliminate a military organization whose constituents, unlike the government troops, knew every mountain pass and strategic spot in this part of the Yellow River valley. In other words, Dachuan posed a serious threat to the Muslim rebels based in the Hezhou region, and their attack against this troublesome village was only a matter of when and how.

But for the Kongs living in the Dachuan area today, talk of 1864 is bound to evoke memories of those Kongs who were converted to Islam, and who are said to have sided with the Muslim rebels from Hezhou against their non-Muslim brethren. But descendants of the Kong Muslims, or Kong Huihui, who now live in a cluster of high mountains across the river,[1] flatly deny that their families took sides against their Dachuan relatives. They explained that their forefathers, as Islamic converts, fled Dachuan in fear of retaliation from government soldiers.[2]

Temple Rebuilt, Destroyed, and Rebuilt Again

About 200 *mu* of farmland owned by the Kong Muslims and villagers who had been killed in 1864 were taken over by the surviving population in Dachuan. Half of this land was managed as corporate property, in the name of the Confucius temple, although the temple itself was not rebuilt until 1935. Its final reconstruction was financed by selling some of this land to private buyers.

When the Communists launched land reform in 1951, the Confucius temple in Dachuan had three large halls used for community meetings and ancestral rituals. A primary school with more than twenty classrooms was situated behind the temple

proper and connected to it. The ancestral rituals, building main-
tenance, and teachers' salaries were funded primarily from 40
mu of farmland still under the temple's control. A team of three
county officials ended the temple management's supervision of
the primary school when land reform was completed in 1953.
They also confiscated the temple's farmland and parceled it out
to land-reform activists. The temple was shut down by the
county government in 1958, and, after the reservoir was built in
1961, the temple's foundations rotted as the water table rose.

The water table, the upper limit of the portion of the ground
saturated with water, may lie near the surface or many meters
below. Under normal circumstances, it drops in periods of
drought or heavy water use, rising again during times of abundant rainfall. When a reservoir is built, however, and begins to
accumulate a thick layer of silt, it blocks up the underground
water passages, pushing the water to the land's surface and thus
damaging crops or houses. Because of the rising water table, Dachuan's Confucius temple and the remaining houses in a higher
section gradually became waterlogged. One household after another was forced to retreat to even higher ground, and finally the
last remnant of Dachuan's original settlement had to be abandoned. The Confucius temple was left to decay amidst the ruins
and sodden fields on the edge of the reservoir. It did not altogether disappear until 1974, when, in response to Chairman
Mao's call to denounce Confucius, the local commune leaders
decided to tear down what remained of the temple and use the
materials to build a warehouse in the commune seat. When the
Kongs learned of this plan, they dismantled the temple themselves and kept its beams, tiles, bricks, and window frames in
the village. These materials were placed under the control of Dachuan's production brigade.

Elaborate ceremonies of ancestor worship began reappearing
in 1984, when a workshop that had been used by local carpenters
was converted into a makeshift shrine. There, "spirit tablets"
were installed for commemorating Confucius and local ancestors. Usually "spirit tablets," *shen wei* or *ling pai* in Chinese

(sometimes translated as "soul tablets"), are made of wood. They have a vertical shape and vary in size. On the front are written the names of the deceased, his or her family's status, and any official titles. The words are written from top to bottom. If known, the hour, day, month, and year of the birth and death of the deceased are noted on the back. When used as the objects of ancestor worship, they are either installed in a communal hall all year round or displayed in the central room of a residence on important ritual days such as the lunar New Year and the tomb-sweeping day of Qingming. The spirit tablets installed at Dachuan's makeshift shrine to commemorate Confucius and local ancestors were made of red paper with the progenitors' names written in black ink. The provisional shrine—dark, small, and shabby—was abandoned when the Kongs built the new Confucius temple, easily the most imposing building in Dachuan.

What the old Confucius temple and its latest reconstruction meant to the Kongs of Dachuan will be examined in greater detail later. The following discussion focuses instead on the Kongs' claim that they are descended from Confucius. We will trace the origins of this claim and what the Kongs choose to remember from a distant past. The purpose of so doing is to set up a broader historical framework in which we can evaluate the ethnographic data collected from contemporary Dachuan.

Laying Claim to an Illustrious Ancestor

Qufu, the hometown of Confucius, is a household name among the Kongs of Dachuan, who regard this ancient town in Shandong province as the site of their "ancestral court" (zu ting). However, only two Kongs from Dachuan had traveled to Qufu between 1949 and 1992. One was a middle-aged man who visited Qufu in 1974, while serving with an army unit stationed near Jinan, the capital of Shandong. The trip was an unpleasant experience; it coincided with the height of Mao's Campaign Against Lin Biao and Confucius. The Qufu he saw was engulfed by the unrelenting roar of political slogans blaring from loudspeakers and an intimidating web of big-character posters on every street. The other visitor was an elderly man whose trip in 1984 was made possible by his youngest son's windfall in a business venture. He arrived just as Qufu was being reopened to the public with great fanfare, as a historic site. In an interview in 1992, this older man said that he was pleasantly surprised during his trip to Qufu by the sight of so many officials, journalists, scholars, and foreign tourists who had gathered in a place that had been excoriated during the Cultural Revolution (1966–76) as "the old hearth of feudalism."

Otherwise, the Kongs of Dachuan have seen Qufu only on television and in magazines. Nevertheless, Qufu is extraordinarily real to their mind's eye. In fact, older villagers discussed Qufu as if they had been there many times. For instance, a roomful of elderly men heard during a banquet that I had spent a week in Qufu in 1984. A watermelon grower immediately asked if I had noticed a gilded couplet at the front gate of the Yansheng Duke's residence. The ducal title of Yansheng, which means "the Honorable Perpetuator of Holy Descent" (*yan sheng gong*), was bestowed by the imperial government on the so-called direct descendants of Confucius through the succession of first sons in each generation. Originally conferred in 1055 by the Emperor Ren Zong of the Song dynasty, the Yansheng Duke's title was passed down thirty generations; it was abolished in 1935 by the Nationalist government.

Seeing that I could not recall the famous couplet, the watermelon grower grinned and proceeded to recite the words: "Sharing national glory is the mansion of the blessed and prominent Duke. As long-lived as heaven is the house of the learned and virtuous saint." He finished the recital with an even broader grin. This man had received only six years of schooling, back in the 1940's.

I was then asked, this time by a retired cook, whether I had visited Nishan, a mountain some thirty kilometers southeast of Qufu. When he heard that I had bypassed this place, thinking there was little to see there, he exclaimed in disbelief, "But the

Confucius Cave is there!" He went on to explain that Confucius was exceptionally ugly at birth: The front of his head was concave, his eyes bulged, his teeth protruded, and his nostrils turned upward. Thinking she had given birth to a monster, his mother abandoned him in a mountain cave. A tiger and an eagle discovered the baby and took it upon themselves to feed and guard him. When his mother heard of these wonders, she realized that her child must have been sent from heaven. She retrieved him from the cave and thereafter devoted herself to his education.

The other elderly men at the banquet also knew this legend. They added bits and pieces of the story that the retired cook failed to mention. They said that the legend of the Confucius Cave was only part of a vast body of Confucius stories they had learned, mainly at the village's primary school, from village storytellers and compilers of local genealogies. When I collected more such stories and compared them with those gathered by two Chinese folklorists from Qufu (Dong & Jiang 1992), I found in them some interesting parallels, namely, similar plots and a tendency to associate Confucius's life with specific sites still observable in his hometown.

These orally transmitted stories are indelibly influenced by two written records. One is a biography of Confucius in the *Records of the Grand Historian* (*shi ji*). Written by the celebrated Sima Qian (see reprint 1972: 905–47) during the reign of Emperor Wu Ti (r. 140–86 B.C.), the biography was quoted by thousands of scholars over centuries and its contents were passed from educated elites to ordinary people. The second source is a variety of illustrated booklets based on the ancient biography. Of these booklets, known as *A Sketch of Holy Traces* (*sheng ji tu*), a stone-engraved edition can be accurately dated to 1592.

Numerous fanciful elements of Confucius's life are included in the biography by Sima Qian and in the illustrated booklets. Yet the content of the orally transmitted tales is even more fantastic and imaginative, revealing a historical process in which the storytellers imposed what was in their own minds on a landscape they thought they were merely describing. Some of these tales emphasize the magical circumstances of Confucius's birth and the sufferings he endured as a child. Others refer to his frustrations as an educator and how the great destiny of his teachings was revealed by such heavenly signs as the appearance of extraordinary rainbows, the sighting of fabulous animals, the inexplicable trembling of mountains, and the altering of waterways. And to return to the story of Confucius's birth and how he was rescued by a tiger and an eagle, the story specifies a tiny cave in Nishan. Though not very impressive-looking, this place has long been a sacred site, known in folklore as *fu zi dong*, or "Confucius Cave" (see Dong & Jiang 1992: 28; Fan 1990: 8; Kong Demao 1984: 18).

Because Confucius and Qufu occupy such a commanding place in the minds of the Kongs of Dachuan, a historical overview of the sage and his birthplace is in order. On this subject, the scholarly works and historical archives in Chinese and Western languages are like a vast sea; no effort is made here to exhaust the available literature. Instead, what is attempted below is an account of the Kong clan named after Confucius. Given the exalted status of Confucius in Chinese history, the development of this clan represents one of the grandest and most inventive uses of kinship in China's political culture.

Confucius and His Descendants in Qufu

According to the *Records of the Grand Historian* (*shi ji*), Confucius was born in 551 B.C. to a family of impoverished nobles and eventually became prime minister of the state of Lu, roughly corresponding to today's Shandong province. But, dismayed by his ruler's dissolute ways, Confucius resigned and devoted himself to teaching his moral precepts to members of noble families in Lu and neighboring states. He died a frustrated man in 478 B.C. without having realized his most cherished ambition of seeing his political ideas implemented.

Nonetheless, three basic elements of his philosophy gradually became embedded in Chinese culture. The first was Confucius's belief that an imperial ruler's political legitimacy should be determined by his ability to create a stable social order and by his compassion for the well-being of his subjects (see Fung 1952; Nivison & Wright 1959; Taylor 1990). The second element was his emphasis on filial piety in the development of the basic microcosm of society—the family (see Creel 1949; Wright 1960). The third was his insistence that the state, society, and the family had to observe the propriety of rituals (see Ebrey 1991a, 1991b; Wilson 1995a); ritual propriety, he held, was particularly important in the management of social ranks and public behavior.

That these ideas attracted many people in imperial China is not surprising. China's history is marked by a succession of wars and famines, repeatedly shattering hopes for stability and predictability. It is against this tumultuous historical backdrop that the Confucian emphasis on the moral basis of political power, on family harmony, and on the ritualization of social hierarchy has had a special appeal. From a historical perspective, Confucianism was sustained by state efforts to hammer out a social order in the midst of upheavals or to safeguard the status quo against the danger-fraught uncertainties of change (see Fairbank 1983: 53–79). This helps explain why the state cult of Confucius was continued by various conquerors of China regardless of their ethnic origins.

The first reliable mention of a regular, state-sponsored cult of Confucius was in A.D. 37. Emperor Guang Wu, founder of the Eastern Han dynasty, visited Shandong in A.D. 29 and ordered a minister to offer sacrifices at Confucius's tomb. In A.D. 37, the same emperor bestowed the title of marquis (hou) on two of the allegedly most direct descendants of Confucius, one of whom was charged with conducting sacrifices to Confucius on behalf of the state. From A.D. 72 to 124, three emperors of the Eastern Han dynasty visited Confucius's hometown to offer sacrifices to the sage (see Shryock [1932] 1966: 99–102). Rulers of succeeding dynasties continued to encourage the worship of Confucius, a practice that rendered great honors to the Kongs of Qufu and lay down the foundation for the growth of a unique descent-based group. It is usually identified in Chinese sources as *kong shi jia zu,* literally "Kong clan."

From Obscurity to Prominence

The Kongs of Qufu did not enjoy high social status until the state cult of Confucius became a regular practice. In 8 B.C., a petition sent to the imperial court by the scholar Mei Fu noted that only Qufu had a Confucius temple and yet the descendants of Confucius remained commoners, lacking the privileges of tax exemption. "It cannot be heaven's intention," Mei Fu declared, "that so great a man should receive honor only from people of so mean a condition" (quoted by Shryock [1932] 1966: 98).

Starting from the year 37, a few Kongs in Qufu were ennobled because of the emerging state cult of Confucius, but they abandoned their hometown in 189 after warfare left Qufu in ruins (Huang Chin-shing 1993: 9). By 221, when order was temporarily restored, Emperor Wen Di of the Wei dynasty had to organize search teams to locate an heir of Confucius from elsewhere to oversee rituals for the sage in Qufu (Huang Chin-shing 1993: 10–11). Subsequent dynastic changes, often marked by lethal conflict, prompted new waves of exodus from Qufu. And when order was restored, imperial edicts were reissued to track down Confucius's descendants.

This lost-and-found pattern is central to the mythologized belief that a direct line of descent through a succession of first sons from the sage progenitor has remained unbroken to the present. This belief is exemplified by the fantastic story of Kong Renyu and Kong Mo, from the late Tang dynasty (923–936). Kong Renyu was the only son in the forty-third generation of the direct Confucian line; Kong Mo was a servant in the Kong household who changed his name from Liu Mo after entering service. At this time, all the family's servants had to take the surname Kong; only after the fall of the Ming dynasty (1644) was the rule changed, barring any servant from being named Kong (Kong Demao 1984: 31). In an attempt to usurp the family's wealth and position during a time of turmoil, it is said, the ambitious Kong Mo murdered the head of the Kong family and then sought to kill the young heir, Kong Renyu, as well. As chance would have it, the boy had gone to visit his wet nurse, known as Mother Zhang. When Kong Mo came to demand the boy, Mother Zhang dressed her own son in Kong Renyu's clothing, allowing him to be murdered in the Kong heir's place. Kong Mo then declared himself to be the direct heir of Confucius. Years later, the story goes, Kong Renyu, who had grown to manhood in Mother Zhang's home, reported Kong Mo's crimes to state authorities. The state reinstalled Kong Renyu as head of the Kong family. He became known as *zhong xing zu*, that is, "Ancestral Line Restorer" (see Kong Decheng 1937; Kong Demao 1984: 30–36; Meng 1990: 79).

This extraordinary tale is recounted in greater detail in the genealogies once kept at the Yansheng Duke's residence. It is obviously impossible to answer conclusively the inevitable question of whether the boy Kong Mo murdered was really Mother Zhang's son or Kong Renyu himself. Despite this problem, the story gave rise to two customs, adhered to until the 1940's. The first involved the Ancestral Line Restorer's gesture of gratitude to Mother Zhang in the form of recognizing the Zhang family as "honorary relatives in perpetuity." This meant that members of the Zhang family were regularly invited to participate in the Kong family's important life-cycle rituals, especially wedding banquets (Kong Demao 1984: 32–36). The second practice was the demarcation of "inner-court Kongs" (*nei yuan kong*) and "outer-court Kongs" (*wai yuan kong*). The former referred to the descendants of Kong Renyu, whereas the latter meant Kong Mo's descendants, who were also labeled "false Kongs" (*wei kong*). A genealogy printed in Qufu in 1937 has an essay entitled "How to Identify False Kongs," illustrated with charts distinguishing the descent lines of Kong Mo, the usurper, and Kong Renyu, the Ancestral Line Restorer.

Even when an undisputed heir had long been available, he

might not be recognized by the emperor of a new dynasty. For example, with the invasion of the Nuzhen (also spelled Juchen) into north China in 1128, the Yansheng Duke, who was patronized by the Han Chinese government, fled with his immediate family to Zhejiang province and settled in the town of Quzhou (Meng 1990; Wilson 1995b; Zhang Weihua 1980). This means that the officially acknowledged direct heirs of Confucius were uprooted and moved to the south. But when the Mongols defeated the Nuzhen regime and went on to attack the Chinese government in the south, vanquishing it in 1282, the Yansheng Duke in Quzhou, Kong Zhu, was forced by the Mongol court to surrender his title (Zhang Weihua 1980: 11–18). The all-powerful Kublai Khan is said to be the one who transferred the title of Yansheng Duke to a man in Qufu, praising him for having dutifully remained behind to guard the grave of Confucius (Meng 1990: 79–80).

Clearly, the claim of the Yansheng dukes and their immediate relatives to lineal descent from Confucius invites skepticism. That it was so resoundingly reiterated over so many centuries required the collaboration of two sets of historical actors. On the one hand, state authorities had an interest in finding trustworthy candidates to supervise the Confucian ritual ceremonies in Qufu. On the other, an ample number of ambitious candidates were eager to lay claim to an illustrious ancestor, especially as this ancestor became increasingly central to China's political culture. The Yansheng dukes, in other words, were political appointees in the merging of two institutions: the private practice of ancestor worship and the state cult of Confucius.

The Kong Clan and Its Economic Base

In addition to official recognition and noble titles, the Yansheng dukes and their immediate kinsmen received from the imperial authorities a vast amount of farmland, handsome stipends, expensive gifts, hereditary laborers, and tax exemptions. As time went by, an originally small band of Kongs gradually developed into what became known as the "Kong clan." To be a member of this clan, one had to be an "inner-court Kong" and to belong to one of "sixty stem households" (*liu shi zong hu*) in Qufu. These households were divided into "big stem households" (*da zong hu*) and "small stem households" (*xiao zong hu*). The big stem households were the residents of twelve splendid mansions in the center of Qufu. The largest mansion was inhabited by the Yansheng Duke, his wife, concubines, and children. The other mansions were occupied by the Yansheng Duke's closest agnates, who usually were prosperous and well educated. The small stem households consisted of the Yansheng Duke's distant agnates, most of whom lived on the outskirts of Qufu as farmers. Many were in fact tenant farmers who worked the "ritual lands" (*ji tian*) given to the Yansheng Duke by the imperial court. These tenant farmers paid rent to the Yansheng Duke but were exempted by the government from corvée labor and military conscription.

The term "household," *hu* in Chinese, does not have a consistent meaning in the Kong genealogies available to us. Evidence of its misleading nature is found in a genealogy compiled by the famous playwright Kong Shangren in 1685. The "big stem households," according to this genealogy, had 670 males. Given that these "households" referred to the residents of the twelve main mansions in Qufu, if the number 670 is anywhere near correct, it makes other claims that each mansion housed an individual household or a conjugal family extremely questionable. The same degree of caution should be applied to the term "small stem households." One of them, containing 668 males, comprised an entire village near Qufu. Another, an "archival household" (*wen xian hu*), had a much smaller family unit, consisting of parents and children who were employed in hereditary positions as archivists at the Yansheng Duke's mansion.

The entire "sixty stem households" were registered in Kong Shangren's genealogy as including nearly 10,000 living persons—8,993 males by my own count of the personal names listed. By 1746, the Kong clan in Qufu had more than 20,000

males. The number exceeded 40,000 by the mid-nineteenth century (He Lingxiu 1981: 486). These figures do not include those
who had migrated, for a variety of reasons, to other parts of
China. The Kongs living outside Qufu had to keep their own
genealogies, and only a few of these genealogies were recognized
by the Yansheng Duke as valid.

One reason for excluding the Kongs outside Qufu was the
Yansheng dukes' cautious attitude toward imperial favors. From
the fifteenth century on, the central government consistently
relied on the Yansheng dukes to determine who was a member
of the Kong clan and thereby eligible for such concessions as reduced taxes and exemptions from corvée labor (Qi 1982: 138–43;
Sun 1982: 66–74). The Yansheng dukes were keenly aware of the
importance of these state favors (He Lingxiu et al. 1981: 31–61).
Fearing that the imperial court might find it too onerous to
maintain these privileges if they were extended to the larger
Kong population, the Yansheng dukes permitted only a small
number of selected Kong communities outside Qufu to enjoy
the imperial largesse (see Zhang Weihua 1980: 123–247). These
communities were required to send their genealogies to Qufu
for validation. Only after the genealogies were stamped with a
Yansheng duke's personal seal and that of the clan council would
government officials recognize the owners of these genealogies
as eligible for corvée exemption and reduced taxes (He Lingxiu
1981: 492). It is unknown whether the Kongs of Dachuan sent
any genealogies to Qufu for verification prior to the 1930's. Of
the older residents I interviewed, none said their forefathers had
ever been spared from corvée labor or taxes.

Even after the Republic was established in 1912, the imperial
favors and honorary titles for the Yansheng Duke and his close
agnates were never formally rescinded. However, local officials
and warlords no longer felt bound by imperial policies. By the
late 1920's, they were aggressively imposing property taxes and
labor conscription on the Kong clan in Qufu (Sun 1982: 705–8).
Meanwhile, the Yansheng Duke's status as China's largest land-
holder was threatened. To promote the worship of Confucius,

the imperial government had given the Kongs enormous tracts of ritual lands, which were scattered over 30 counties in five prosperous provinces. The ritual lands in Shandong alone totaled 323,802 *mu*, roughly 60,000 acres, of high-quality farmland, according to a 1919 registry (Qi 1982: 4; Sun 1982: 717). In December 1928, senior officials of the Nationalist government proposed nationalizing the Kong clan's ritual lands (Sun 1982: 715–19). When the proposal was made public, in October 1929, the clan elders panicked. To prevent the loss of the ritual lands, they attempted to rally opposition to the plan and issued a desperate statement in the name of the Yansheng Duke, a man named Kong Decheng, who now lives in Taiwan. The statement, published in newspapers, attacked the proposal as a violation of private property and a threat to the state cult of Confucius (Qi 1982: 212; Sun 1982: 721–22).

Finally, Finance Minister H. H. Kong intervened. As a kinsman of Kong Decheng and brother-in-law of Chiang Kai-shek, he supported the Kongs in Qufu with the result that the proposal to confiscate the Kongs' ritual lands was rejected at the Cabinet level (Sun 1982: 719–23). But the publicity proved damaging, for it brought into the open the issue of whether the imperial title of Yansheng Duke should be maintained under a republic. In 1935, bending to official and popular pressure, Kong Decheng gave up the title. But only after the Communists occupied Qufu did he surrender the ritual lands to the Nationalist government, in what was by then a purely symbolic gesture of political loyalty.

Dachuan's Connection to Qufu

It was amid these assaults on its traditional privileges that the council of the Kong clan decided to recognize Kongs in other parts of China by including them in a new genealogy. In 1930, the clan council issued public notices urging the Kongs scattered throughout China to send genealogical registers to Qufu, as the first phase of the planned reworking of the clan's genealogies (Kong Demao 1984). The Kongs in the Dachuan area were among those who responded (Kong Qinghui 1948: 24), subsequently obtaining recognition by Qufu as part of the Kong line of descent. Judging by the place-names listed in the revised clan genealogy, which was published in 1937, the Kong diaspora was widely dispersed, ranging from the border with what was then the Soviet Union in the northeast to the Pearl River delta in China's deep south, and from the affluent coastal regions in the east to the windswept and barren Qinghai-Tibet plateau in the northwest.

In her memoir of life in what was arguably China's most privileged family over time, Kong Demao, the elder sister of Kong Decheng, recalls that in 1928, when her brother was still a child, their late father's first wife, Madam Tao, discussed with clan elders how to bring the clan genealogy up to date. In October 1930, the decision to include Kongs in other parts of China was finalized, and a central genealogical office was opened in Qufu (Kong Demao 1984: 24–26). Because of Kong Decheng's youth, the genealogical project was headed by Kong Chuanpu, chairman of the clan council and chief assistant to the young Yansheng Duke.

To publicize this ambitious project, notices were placed in newspapers, and regional "genealogical bureaus" (*pu guan*) were established. Through these regional bureaus, the central office sent the Kong diaspora letters with detailed instructions on how to compile the local genealogical records to be sent to Qufu. One of these letters was sent to Lanzhou and relayed to the Kongs in Yongjing county. Four people—two from Dachuan—were immediately entrusted with drawing up a local register. When it was completed, Kong Qinghui, a rich merchant and an important figure among the Kongs in Yongjing, found it necessary to have this register revised with the help of hired scholars from Lanzhou, for it had not been written in the style and format stipulated by the central genealogical office in Qufu. After sending the polished version to Qufu, Kong Qinghui received a letter of acknowledgment from the clan council, which stated that this local register would be included in the clan genealogy.[3]

It should be mentioned here that Kong Qinghui was originally from Xiaochuan, a Kong village that had been settled in 1585 by people belonging to the third segment of the local Kong lineage. His involvement in the compilation of the genealogical register in response to Qufu's request was in part motivated by his desire to bolster the prestige of Xiaochuan. This can be seen in his memoir (Kong Qinghui 1948), which specifies that Xiaochuan alone financed the compilation of the genealogical register. During interviews in 1992, this claim was fiercely disputed by many elderly Kongs in Dachuan.

In the spring of 1937, Kong Qinghui traveled to north China on business and stopped off in Qufu to see if he could obtain a copy of the clan genealogy to bring home to Gansu. But the genealogy was still being printed. By the time he completed his business trip, the Sino-Japanese war had broken out and he was unable to return to Qufu. He went back to Gansu empty-handed.

Kong Qinghui returned to Qufu on May 26, 1948. He was warmly received by six clan elders; the day after his arrival, a banquet was given in his honor. The Yansheng Duke was not on hand because he had already left Qufu, fearing the imminent takeover of north China by the Communists. Toward the end of the banquet, a messenger came in to report that Communist troops had advanced into adjacent Sishui county (Kong Qinghui 1948: 11–12). Having obtained a complete copy of the new clan genealogy, Kong Qinghui visited Qufu's Confucius temple. He left the next day, just hours before Qufu and a brigade of Nationalist troops were besieged by the Communists.

To protect the historic town, the commander of the Communist troops gave strict orders to his men to refrain from using heavy artillery. Twelve days later, the Communists allowed the besieged Nationalist soldiers to leave Qufu by its south gate, then gunned them down in an open field (Kong Fanyin 1992: 388). As soon as Qufu fell to the Communists, the council of clan elders was disbanded and a work team of Communist officials entered the immense Yansheng Duke's residence to make an inventory of its property and the cultural relics in the nearby Confucius temple (Kong Fanyin 1992: 388–89). In retrospect, the banquet Kong Qinghui attended might well have been the clan council's last supper. He was no doubt the last person to obtain a copy of the new genealogy before the clan council was abolished.

Comprising 108 volumes and more than 9,000 pages (Kong Decheng 1937), the genealogy took seven years to complete. The genealogical office in Qufu alone employed 64 people as scribes, accountants, archival assistants, and proofreaders. The project was entirely funded by contributions from Kongs throughout China. A total of 1,704 individual volumes of the genealogy were distributed, mostly through the mail. The postal service refused, however, to mail any complete sets of the genealogy, since each set weighed more than fifty pounds (Kong Qinghui 1948:23). Thus, 290 complete sets had to be carried out of Qufu by representatives of their intended recipients. The set taken by Kong Qinghui was carried out of Qufu in two rickshaws, transferred by several porters onto a train, and then loaded onto a Lanzhou-bound passenger airplane.

The genealogy so laboriously brought to Gansu was burned by a college-based Red Guard organization in Lanzhou at the beginning of the Cultural Revolution in 1966. One of the original sets, however, is available at Harvard University's Yenching Library. In this genealogy, the Kong diaspora is identified as "migration households" (*liu yu hu*). They are divided into ten regional branches, with each branch identified by a place name. The presence of Kongs in places outside Qufu is related to a long process of migration prompted by official appointments, military invasions, economic reversals, and natural disasters. The ten branches of the "migration households" are named for the initial resettlement sites. For example, the Kongs of Dachuan, whose ancestors are said to have first resettled in Guangdong in south China before moving to the northwest, are identified as belonging to the *ling nan pai*, or "the Guangdong branch."

Each regional branch of the Kong clan must once have been a property-sharing lineage within the same locality. The Guangdong branch, for example, is identified in the 1937 genealogy as originating in Pinglincun (Flat Forest Village), Baochang county, Guangdong. This original base for the Guangdong branch is said to have been founded by Kong Changbi, a member of the forty-first generation of the Kong clan who assumed an important military post in the southern city of Guangzhou in 900 (Kong Decheng 1937; Kong Xianmin 1905). Kong Changbi's descendants are said to have moved later to three other places in Guangdong. One of these was the city of Huizhou, 120 kilometers east of Guangzhou.

The Kong Migration to Gansu

From Huizhou, a man named Kong Jiaxing migrated to Gansu in an unknown year during the period of Mongol rule there (1271–1368). Seven generations later, one of his descendants, Kong Gongyou, went to live in a mountain village outside Lanzhou. From there, Kong Gongyou's four sons settled in the village of Dachuan in the Yellow River valley of what is today's Yongjing county. The exact date of the Kong migration to Dachuan is not known. But a property contract preserved in a 1905 genealogy of the Kongs living in Yongjing shows that in 1501, two Kongs bought a large tract of farmland about ten kilometers east of Dachuan. It is thus safe to assume that at least some Kongs were already settled in the Dachuan area at the turn of the sixteenth century. The 1905 genealogy just mentioned contains twelve major land purchases from 1501 to 1731. The signatures in these documents are the names of individual buyers. The place names for these purchased fields cover an extensive stretch of fields along the river valley of Yongjing county.

By the turn of the twentieth century, a narrow gorge locally known as Liujiaxia began to assume great importance in the economic life of the Kongs. With a sharp increase in the domestic and foreign demand for animal pelts, wool, and logs from the Qinghai-Tibetan highlands, Liujiaxia became a key point in the transport of goods along the Yellow River. On the downstream flow to the city of Lanzhou, the rafts—made from inflated animal skins and stacked with sheep's wool—had to be guided by local navigators familiar with the rapids, undercurrents, and rocks in the narrow gorge. As for other kinds of rafts, made of dozens and sometimes hundreds of logs lashed together, they were taken apart to pass through the gorge of Liujiaxia. Below the gorge, they were reassembled to continue their voyage downstream. A local chamber of commerce was formed around the wool trade and logging industry. Most of the merchants in this chamber of commerce were surnamed Kong.

The prestige of the Kong lineage in Yongjing was bolstered not only by the wealth of some of its members but also by their rapport with local officials. This is revealed in the 1905 genealogy, which has a collection of texts in praise of the Kong lineage's glory and history. Among the authors of these texts were six county magistrates.

It should be mentioned here that some members of the Kong lineage were deeply involved with three of Yongjing county's largest religious societies, which in 1949 had a total of 10,289 registered members. Two of these societies were headquartered in the Dachuan area and controlled by people surnamed Kong. As we shall see in the next chapter, the Kong connection with these powerful religious societies became a grave source of political troubles for Dachuan when the Communists took power.

3

Memory of Revolutionary Terror

Invented Tradition and Maoist Campaigns

The story of the Kong clan, especially its claim of descent from an illustrious progenitor, has evoked numerous studies of the invented aspects of tradition and the manipulative uses of historical accounts (see Handler & Linnekin 1984: 273–90; Hanson 1989: 890–902; Hobsbawm & Ranger 1984; Moore 1986, 1987). These studies remind us that making the past serve the present requires the constant employment of cultural inventions to turn a combination of hallowed myths, historical distortions, and imagined realities into collective beliefs (see also Diamond 1988; Herzfeld 1985, 1986; Hill 1988; Rambo 1990). No tradition is invented overnight, however, and whatever is invented must be at least somewhat compatible with cultural conventions and existing social practices. Subject to challenge and negotiation, its meanings are necessarily flexible in its early presentation to the public. An invented tradition can have little public appeal or authority unless it is integrated with popular beliefs about the past. Once embedded in a society's memory, it represents the absolute truth for many members of that society. More than anything, its efficacy and durability hinge on social organization.

What a viable invention gains from social organization is "a persistent framework into which all detailed recall must fit" (Bartlett [1932] 1954:296). To analyze this "persistent framework" is to ask these questions: Who is doing the inventing? Why is it being done? What methods are employed? And how does the invention interact with conventional ideas and customs? It is with these questions in mind that I take up in this chapter the state-organized violence in Dachuan during the Maoist era. The discussion below will first examine the circumstances surrounding the closing and subsequent destruction of Dachuan's old Confucius temple. We will then look at the reconstruction of this religious site with special attention to the remembrance of political terror and the highly inventive, even calculated, methods adopted by the temple managers to direct the temple's rebuilding and subsequent temple-based ceremonies.

Dachuan Under Attack

Before dawn on a frigid December morning in 1950, Dachuan was besieged by a regiment of the People's Liberation Army (PLA). This military action came in response to reports that a rebellion was being organized by several Kongs who held key positions in what many China scholars call "secret societies" (see Chesneaux 1971; Naquin 1976; Lieberthal 1973:242–66; Perry 1980; Wakeman 1972). All exits from the village were sealed off as soldiers went from one compound to the next, searching for weapons. After a full cartload of daggers, spears, swords, hunting guns, and old muskets was hauled away, a mass rally was staged and about 50 local people were paraded onto an improvised stage. These villagers, whom the government accused of being affiliated with "reactionary religious associations" (*fan dong hui dao men*), were warned by military and government officials that any misconduct on their part would meet with severe penalties. Three Kongs, key members of a semireligious and highly militant group known as the Big Sword Society (*da dao hui*), were escorted out of Dachuan, and beheaded.

The search for weapons and the executions at Dachuan heralded the new government's crackdown on religious societies. Five months later, an "investigation-and-registration" campaign (*ging cha deng ji*) identified more than 11,500 people in Yongjing county as members of "reactionary religious associations." The largest such organizations were the Tao of Conscience (*liang xin dao*) and the Society of Ethics (*dao de hui*). The former had 4,373 registered members and the latter 3,739. The Tao of Conscience, also known as the Confucius and Mencius Society (*kong meng hui*), had close ties to the Kong lineage. It was headed mostly by people surnamed Kong, three of whom were from Dachuan. Ten leaders of this society were hounded to death in the investigation-and-registration campaign. Of the three Kongs from Dachuan, one committed suicide and two perished in a labor camp. The Society of Ethics was also connected to the Kong lineage. It was founded by Kong Fanzheng in 1916, and its most loyal followers were from the Dachuan area. There were 28 shrines dedicated to this organization throughout the valley area of Yongjing. Its headquarters were at a shrine known as the "Goodwill Preservation Altar" (*bao shan tan*), located in a Kong village near Dachuan.

Both the Tao of Conscience and the Society of Ethics had been proclaiming, since 1947, that a catastrophe was imminent and that salvation could be achieved by joining their organizations. While these apocalyptic warnings disturbed the newly founded Communist government of Yongjing, local officials were more worried by a third organization—the Big Sword Society. A handful of Kongs from the Dachuan area held senior positions in this organization, which had 2,565 members, mostly armed with swords, knives, and old rifles.

Local officials suspected that the Big Sword Society was gearing up for all-out rebellion, and this fear appeared confirmed by, among other things, a street brawl in Dachuan. As older villagers recounted it, several days before the PLA siege in December 1950, a Communist official passed through Dachuan. A member of the local Big Sword Society accosted him and cursed him for arrogance. The two men came to blows, but because the official's wife was from Dachuan, bystanders intervened in his defense and broke up the fight. The Big Sword member, furious, shouted that he and his society brothers would kill not only the official's family but other Communists in the township. This threat alarmed the local government, which called in the PLA soldiers.

Before the PLA strike on Dachuan, a less dramatic assault was waged against the village's *bao jia* system, the local security and administration structure left over from the days of Nationalist rule. Under this system, which resembled forms of military organization (see Kuhn 1970: 24–28), the village was divided into six security units, each controlled by a "unit commander" (*fen guan*), whose work was dictated by a "security chief" (*bao zhang*). As local agents of the state, these people were responsible for military conscription, tax collection, and implementing other policy directives. After the Communists took power in Yongjing in August 1948, a "Poor Peasants Association" (*pin xie*) was established to replace the *bao jia* system. Eight villagers who had been in charge of the *bao jia* system from 1938 to 1948 were barred from leaving the village without official permission.[1]

Landlords and well-to-do residents were the next group targeted after the PLA action against the secret society members in Dachuan. Land reform was introduced there in September 1951 and completed in June 1953. As in other parts of China, the first step in land reform was the assignment of class identities (see Crook & Crook 1959, 1979; Friedman, Pickowicz, & Selden 1991; Hinton 1966; Shue 1980; Vogel 1969: 27–62; C. K. Yang 1959). In Dachuan, five households were labeled as landlords and nine households as rich peasants, both of which were considered "exploiting classes." The average landholding of these households was 326 *mu*, roughly 56 acres. One landlord and two rich peasants were sent from Dachuan to reform institutions, where they later died. Another 45 key members of these households were deprived of much of their land and were forced to live under the surveillance of the Communist-appointed village cadres.

The Temple's Decline

Perhaps the most fundamental change in the village's social order was the collapse of what anthropologists call "lineage elders" (see e.g., Freedman 1966: 19–44; Hu 1948; Potter & Potter 1990: 8–11). As explained earlier, the Kong lineage in this area had four major segments, which in Dachuan were broken down into eight smaller divisions. Before land reform, each of these divisions occupied a specific neighborhood, usually centered on an important estate and bearing such names as "old fortress" (*lao bu zi*), "high street" (*shang hang dao*) or "tile-roofed house" (*wa fang*). In an overlap with the *bao jia* system, communal affairs at these neighborhoods were handled jointly by big landowners, village administrators, men who were literate or had especially forceful personalities, and experts in ritual and genealogy. Nonetheless, each neighborhood had but one nominal supervisor, known as the "neighborhood patriarch" (*hang dao lao zhe*). These people, in turn, were overseen by the "lineage chief" (*da jia zhang*). He was the one who, for example, determined whether a special tassel of willow boughs should be used to lash a wrongdoer's bared back. This instrument of punishment was called *jia fa*, literally "family law," and whenever it was to be applied, a bell in the Confucius temple was rung to call people to witness the beating. By the late 1930's, the practice of public beating had died out, but the lineage chief and his assistants continued to make their influence felt in their roles as arbiters of civil disputes, organizers of community-wide ceremonies, and, above all, as managers of the Confucius temple.

An examination of the lineage elders' backgrounds indicates that not all of them were from well-to-do families. Nor were they necessarily senior by age or generational rank. Rather, achieving prominence in the local lineage organization appeared to depend on four other criteria: moral authority, political influence, ritual expertise, and personal charisma. The first was determined by public perceptions of a man's ability to handle communal affairs with reasonable fairness. The second often was gained through the sponsorship of rich and prominent members of the community who preferred to shape events from behind the scenes. The third derived from public trust in a man's ability to guide ritual ceremonies. The fourth was related to qualities of character, which might be defined by known acts of heroism or from literary skills.

But under Communist rule, these people's prestige plummeted with the erosion of their accustomed sources of political backing, their influence as mediators in disputes, and their supervision of communal ritual affairs. This decline started with their loss of control over the primary school and the farmland attached to the Confucius temple.

The sequence by which the influential groups of Dachuan were targeted by the new government for political persecution and economic degradation suggests considerable premeditation and careful execution. First, the *bao jia* system was eradicated, followed by the suppression of secret societies. Next, the most prosperous households came under attack. Finally, lineage organization and ritual management were crippled. In accordance with the military tactics advocated by Mao Zedong, the new government overcame the range of potential adversaries in Dachuan by isolating and striking down one targeted group after another.

The phased tightening of controls over Dachuan, with violence when deemed necessary, underscored the Communist government's wariness toward potential challenges from large religious or descent-based organizations.[2] To avert trouble from a multicommunity lineage like the Kongs, Dachuan, as the lineage center, was subjected to especially close supervision. The revolutionary terror took an immediate and heavy toll on the community. Not only was the traditional structure of local governance destroyed, but the long-standing networks of communal support were dismantled. Although the number of people in the village who were directly attacked was limited, the overall impact was devastating. Implementing the Maoist theory of class struggle resulted in a radical overturning of power rela-

tions. Former community leaders were subordinated to those
who once had been of inferior rank. At the same time, the local
kinship structure was fractured when social distinctions were
redrawn along Communist definitions of socioeconomic "class
identities" (cheng fen) and politically determined "family backgrounds" (chu shen). Close relatives became distant co-villagers
once individuals were stigmatized as "class enemies," "counterrevolutionaries," or "sons and daughters of landlords and rich
peasants." The scope of moral reasoning based on traditional
ethical standards was drastically reduced as public positions fell
into the hands of political activists whose solutions to local
problems hinged on their deference to an obviously very effective force—the new Communist regime.

The Shutdown of the Temple

From mid-August to late September 1958, during the high
tide of the Great Leap Forward, police and militia forces rounded
up 855 people in Yongjing county. In documents I examined at
the Yongjing county archives, the roundup is identified as "the
1958 manhunt." Twenty-one of the people arrested were executed right away. The others, mostly former landlords, leaders
of secret societies, and people with Nationalist ties, were detained in the offices of the county and district (commune)
governments. They were given stern warnings about the importance of compliance with the Great Leap Forward and the collectivization drive. They were not released until the people's commune system was in place at the village level.

The arrests and killings were accompanied by an "Anti–
Feudal Privilege Campaign." The term "feudal privilege" refers
to what the county officials regarded as remnants of the old order, especially in the realm of religion. In the first few years under Communist rule, leaders of larger religious societies were
eradicated, but many middle-ranking society members were
spared. Many of the survivors engaged in clandestine activities
in smaller religious groups attached to temples honoring various

deities and community patron gods. These people were under suspicion as possible forces of resistance to collectivization.

As a result of the Anti–Feudal Privilege Campaign, the county's major Taoist, Buddhist, and popular deities' temples were dismantled. Only a nationally renowned group of Buddhist shrines built into mountain caves was spared. Materials taken from the dismantled temples were used to construct bridges, schools, and irrigation facilities. By a government decree, smaller shrines and ancestor halls at the village level were closed or converted to secular use. Dachuan's Confucius temple was sealed off at this time.

The arrests and the shutdown of religious structures through-out Yongjing were in part a response to the religious basis of an armed uprising in nearby Dongxiang county, where, in mid-August 1958, Muslim imams from local mosques organized their followers to resist collectivization. An unknown number of government officials were killed, including the Dongxiang county magistrate. The rebellion was soon put down by a PLA brigade.

Based on interviews and official documents, I found that at least ten Kongs in Dachuan alone were executed or hounded to death in the period between the PLA assault in late 1950 and the founding of the people's commune in 1958. During the same period, 121 people in Dachuan were classified as "bad elements" and "class enemies." These included two former lineage elders, nine "security chiefs," five "practitioners of feudal superstition," four low-ranking former Kuomintang officers, two school teachers, 48 adults from "landlord" and "rich peasant" house-holds, and 51 members of religious societies. The penalties they suffered included long-term imprisonment, forced labor, police surveillance, loss of property, and prohibitions on travel.

The Temple's Destruction

The collapse of the Kong lineage institutions and Dachuan's old social order were followed by continued political campaigns aimed at eliminating the last fragments of the old society. For example, geomancy and shamanistic healing were still secretly practiced until at least the early 1960's, but once the Cultural Revolution was launched in 1966 even such activities became virtually impossible to carry on. The extent of the Cultural Revolution's attack on traditional culture can be seen in the public destruction, often by fire, of religious implements. Such objects as almanacs (*huang li*), prayer books (*jing ben*), divination compasses (*luo pan*), and fortune-telling sticks (*ming qian*) were confiscated by village cadres from their hiding places, usually with the help of informers. At the beginning of 1974, the one tangible vestige of the old culture that could be seen in Dachuan was the empty and waterlogged Confucius temple. But even its days were numbered.

At a conference in March 1973, Mao said it was necessary to criticize Lin Biao and Confucius. Lin had been Mao's designated successor but later clashed with him and in 1971 reportedly died in an airplane crash on his way to the Soviet Union after an assassination plot against Mao failed. The curious inclusion of Confucius as a target in this campaign, formally launched in early 1974, is now generally interpreted as an attack on Premier Zhou Enlai, who, following Lin Biao's death, attempted to rehabilitate senior officials sacked by Mao at the onset of the Cultural Revolution. During this campaign, says Roderick MacFarquhar (1990), Confucius was denounced for having urged the restoration of the political institutions and rituals of the ancient Zhou dynasty by reviving the noble families whose lines of succession had broken down by his time. "This was an oblique but unmistakable critique of Zhou's rehabilitation of senior cadres, particularly clear to those who knew that this passage referred to the actions of Zhou's namesake, the great twelfth century B.C. statesman, the Duke of Zhou" (MacFarquhar 1990: 550–51). With its bizarre linkage of Confucius, Lin Biao, and Zhou Enlai, this campaign involved millions of people, from schoolchildren, officials, and intellectuals to workers, farmers, and soldiers. At the village level, perhaps the most affected were those who bore the surname of Confucius, Kong. Certainly that was the case in Dachuan.

In February 1974, officials held a series of meetings in the Yongjing county seat at which they planned mass rallies to criticize Lin Biao and Confucius in all the county's communes. According to the "Anti–Lin Biao and Confucius Campaign" bulletins preserved in the Yongjing county archives, a work team of fourteen cadres from the county's Department of People's Armed Forces (*wu zhuang bu*) was sent to the commune affiliated with Dachuan. These officials called up more than a hundred local militiamen armed with automatic rifles in case the Kongs put up violent resistance to the campaign.

The commune's administrative offices were located in Zhongzhuang, a Kong village adjacent to Dachuan. In this village, the work team and militiamen posted 150 political slogans on walls of residential buildings, set up 34 blackboard notices, and painted 26 political caricatures, all targeting Lin Biao and Confucius. These deeds were dutifully recorded in a thick official file, alongside another report that concedes that the campaign was sabotaged and that it was difficult to mobilize the local masses to criticize Confucius.

The sabotage consisted of a few instances of political slogans being ripped off walls and blackboards being knocked down. No culprit was identified, although the Kongs were immediately suspected. While the hunt for saboteurs was under way, a decision was taken on a plan already under discussion by the work team and commune officials: the Confucius temple in Dachuan would be leveled to remove the last material evidence of Confucianism from public sight. It was also decided that the militiamen should take what was left of the temple to the commune seat to use in building a warehouse. When word of this plan reached Dachuan, a group of elderly men urged the village cadres to tear down the temple first so the Kongs could at least keep the building materials for themselves. Before the commune leaders could send militiamen to Dachuan, the temple was quietly dismantled and its parts hidden, intermingled with construction materials kept in a workshop used by the village's carpenters. The commune's demand that the temple's building materials be surrendered was rebuffed by the village cadres, who claimed they did not know who dismantled the temple or where the materials were.

This incident further exasperated the work team and commune leaders, who had lost an opportunity to dismantle the temple in dramatic fashion to highlight their devotion to the campaign. In retaliation, they brought a selected group of middle-school students to the site of the ruined temple and instructed them to build a gravelike mound from rubble. The children were then led in the shouting of political slogans directed against this makeshift symbol of Confucianism, in a public ritual of humiliation. Many of the students who participated in the rally were themselves Kongs, Dachuan's village cadres were required to attend, and bystanders were from the community.

In interviews in Dachuan during my fieldwork, informants said that no one from Dachuan had dared to object to the ritual of humiliation. The work team and commune officials, backed up by a hundred armed militiamen in the commune seat less than a mile away, were being deliberately provocative and looking for any excuse to take harsher action.

Finding Memories of Persecution

How do the Kongs recall those years of political persecution? And what lessons have the local villagers drawn from these experiences? In my effort to find answers to these questions, I set about constructing an outline of major local events related to national political campaigns launched by the Communist Party from 1949 to 1976. At the county archives, I was able to use some official files to compile a partial reconstruction of Dachuan's recent history. Interviews were conducted thereafter to flesh out the documentary material, a task that proved far more difficult than expected.

Although the village interviews filled in some gaps in the official files, they were marked by evasions and silences. The oral narratives of the village's political history were frustratingly fragmentary. In fact, village informants were reluctant to talk about the political campaigns prior to the Cultural Revolution because, even under the post-Mao leadership, the land reform, persecution of rural elites, suppression of local cults, and attacks on semi-secret and armed religious societies still cannot be criticized; they are still justified by the government as important and positive steps to reform Chinese society. In the official history of Chinese socialism from 1949 to Mao's death in 1976, only the Cultural Revolution can be condemned.

So people who had been persecuted before the Cultural Revolution usually resorted in interviews to what might be called a "vindicative strategy," in which they frequently protested that they had been wrongly labeled as enemies of the people, rather than question the premises of the persecution. Some tried to convince the listener that they had been framed when they were classified as counterrevolutionaries. Others complained that they had been classified as landlords even though their families had owned only a small plot of land. A villager described in detail the fluctuations in his family's landholding over five generations, just to make it clear to me that his father was mistakenly identified as an "upper-middle peasant."

After these explanations, informants would proceed to their experience of political persecution, not in terms of whether it should have happened, to them or anyone else, but why they personally did not deserve it. They were essentially saying that the political campaigns against landowners, religious leaders, local agents of the Nationalist regime, and organizers of secret societies might have been necessary, but that they themselves had been erroneously targeted. The initial interviews designed to investigate Dachuan's political history from a personal perspective were not very successful.

After a longer stay in the village, I sensed that my informants found it puzzling that an outsider, particularly an urban scholar, could be interested in their accounts of village life under Mao.

Furthermore, many were convinced that no outsider could appreciate the complexities of local events. Above all, they were clearly afraid that any information they gave me might be misused, disrupting their relations with other people. To escape this impasse, I abandoned the direct approach and paid more attention to subtexts in my informants' narratives. By subtexts, I mean random but revealing comments, indirect references, passing assertions, and private gossip. Once I began piecing these together, the fragmentary elements characteristic of oral narratives began to shed important light on a number of matters, including the highly unconventional arrangement of spirit tablets in the rebuilt Confucius temple's main structure—the Monumental Hall of Great Accomplishment.

Changing Spirit Tablets

Inside this newly constructed hall are five spirit tablets, made from willow wood painted teal blue and framed in black. Their inscriptions are in gold. The tablet in the center, three meters high and less than a meter wide, is devoted to Confucius. It stands on a brick platform, veiled by colorful silk screens and surrounded by small vases of paper flowers. It reads: "Spirit Tablet of Confucius, the Eminent Prince of Literary Excellence, and the First Teacher of Great Accomplishment."

In front of Confucius's tablet is an offering table, flanked by two wooden pillars bearing the lines of a couplet in fine calligraphy. Hanging from the pillars' crossbeam are three red banners with embroidered borders and hand-written statements of veneration for Confucius. Above the banners and below the building's highest cross-beam is a conspicuously empty space, reserved for a large wooden plaque that will bear an inscription by Kong Decheng, the seventy-sixth-generation heir of Confucius and the last Yansheng Duke, who is still living in Taiwan.[3] The spirit tablet displayed to the right of the offering table is devoted to four ancient scholars, Yan Hui, Zeng Zi, Zi Si, and Meng Ke, who were acclaimed followers of Confucius. The spirit tablet on the left is devoted to "Seventy-Two Early Worthies," who were supposedly taught by Confucius himself.[4] These two tablets are enshrined on their own separate platforms, also shaded by silk screens and surrounded by paper flowers.[5]

Against the side walls are two plain tables. On one is displayed the "Spirit Tablet of the Fifty-Second-Generation Ancestor Xin Ke Gong, Who Came to Gansu"; on the other is the "Spirit Tablet of the Fifty-Eighth-Generation Ancestor Yu Hou, and His Four Sons: Yan Zheng, Yan Kui, Yan Bin, and Yan Rong, Who Came to Dachuan."

The significance of these tablets is that they bring together two very different categories of people—ancestors of the Kongs but also ancient scholars unrelated to the Kongs—in an arrangement that breaks sharply with traditional practice. According to the temple watchman, the new temple differs from both the old temple that was shut down in 1958 and the provisional shrine set up in 1984. For example, in the old temple and the provisional shrine, the spirit tablet of Confucius was inscribed with the honorary titles of "Eminent Prince of Literary Excellence" and "First Teacher of Great Accomplishment," but also "Holy Ancestor" (*sheng zu*). On the tablet in the new temple, "Holy Ancestor" is omitted.

Moreover, in the old temple and the provisional shrine, the table for Confucius was surrounded by spirit tablets for local ancestors. Among these was the Kong Jiaxing, who migrated to Lanzhou from Guangdong province, and whose descendants later moved to a village named Yan Jiawan (Yan Family Terrace) and finally settled in Dachuan. But in the new temple, tablets for these ancestors have been relegated to the sides. And the tablet for Confucius is immediately flanked by the tablets for the followers of Confucius. Only one of these was related to the Kongs—a man named Zi Si, who is said to have been Confucius's grandson.

Another difference: the old temple and the provisional shrine were clearly monuments to Kong ancestors. In contrast, the fourteen men who had banded together in 1985 to build the new temple maintained in interviews that its purpose was to provide a place for the broader public to honor the founders of Chinese culture. In their capacity as the temple's managers, they insisted that it was not exclusively a Kong ancestral hall.

To understand why the Kongs chose to integrate spirit tablets for outsiders with those of their own ancestors and to give these ancestors second billing, and why they seemed to feel it necessary, in public at least, to redefine the temple's nature, we must examine the complex process by which the temple managers attempted to reconstruct the temple's history, to recover whatever remained from the old temple, and to devise appropriate rituals. This examination begins with a discussion of cohort analysis and then traces the way the fear of political persecution shaped a series of cultural inventions.

Generational Cohorts

Cohort analysis was initially developed in demography and later applied in sociology and social history. In its demographic origins, it focused on people born around the same time. As employed by sociologists and social historians, it was combined with notions of historical generations, namely, those people who share historical moments that forge their identity.

Renato Rosaldo, who applied cohort analysis to the study of collective memory among the Ilongot of northern Luzon, in the Philippines, explains the usefulness of this technique: "The point of entry in cohort analysis is an inquiry into the extent to which a number of individuals have become self-conscious about their identity as a group in the face of life chances terribly different in appearance from those of their elders and their juniors. The formation of such a group, indeed, the very shape of its collective identity, is based initially on a shared sense of life possibilities and later on the shared knowledge of and reflection about life outcomes" (Rosaldo 1980: 111). Put another way, the cultural dispositions of generational cohorts are molded by experiencing events peculiar to the historical time framed by the dates of their birth and death.

Another helpful application of cohort analysis, this one in the field of social memory research, is a study by Howard Schuman and Jacqueline Scott (1989: 359–81). These researchers surveyed a national sample of adult Americans who were asked to name and describe twelve significant "national or world events or changes over the past fifty years." The Schuman-Scott study is meant to elucidate the relations between generational effects, life course, and collective memory. A central hypothesis tested in this study is whether historical events and social changes have a "maximum impact in terms of memorableness" upon age-set cohorts if they experienced these events when they were still adolescents and young adults. In their inquiry, Schuman and Scott draw on ideas of Halbwachs, especially his crucial distinction between autobiographic and historical memory. The former is seen as more consequential, richer, and personally more meaningful than the latter. In accord with the concept of collective memory developed by Halbwachs, Schuman and Scott ask whether autobiographic memories of directly experienced events do indeed have deeper impact than events of which people have merely read or heard about. They found that most of the twelve major events named by the interviewees "refer back disproportionally to a time when the respondents were in their teens or early twenties." This finding suggests that memories of important political or social events are strongly related to age, in particular to young adulthood. It also echoes a number of other studies supporting the Halbwachsian proposition that crucial public events leave deep imprints in the minds of direct participants, especially when they are in the early stages of developing an adult identity (see, e.g., Brown & Kulik 1982; Rosaldo 1980; Winograd & Killinger 1983).

A basic problem with this type of analysis is the assumption that the experience shared by age-set groups in early adulthood has an intrinsic effect on memory. It is taken for granted that direct participation in events is correlated with the ability to recall those events. Ulric Neisser (1982) has questioned this assumption by suggesting that the preservation of cohort memories may result from frequent rehearsal of memories and retelling of tales. He emphasizes that the importance of a cohort experience is not always apparent at the time, but only established later. The rehearsal of cohorts' memories, he points out, is often overlooked by researchers. Consequently, the importance of memory repetition, which can be crucial to the ability to recall an event, has received little study.

The Dachuan material certainly supports the validity of Neisser's observation. As will become clear, cohort memories played a vital role in the rebuilding of Dachuan's Confucius temple. But it must be noted that the cohorts in question are a group of elderly men whose contributions to the temple's reconstruction were shaped by a process in which their own memories were modified by institutional interests.

Temple Managers

The fourteen men most responsible for building and managing the new temple are known locally as "vow-takers" (yuan zhu). In this case, the vow was their promise to construct a good temple and to manage it well thereafter. It was taken at a meeting of representatives of Kong villages from Yongjing county in September 1986. Except for the "chief vow-taker" (da yuan zhu), who was in his late thirties at the time of this meeting, the other vow-takers were all in their late sixties and early seventies. Five of the fourteen vow-takers were from Dachuan and served as the temple's core administrators. The "chief vow-taker," the only young person, was the village's head from 1986 to 1988. Under him was the "deputy chief vow-taker" (er yuan zhu). A veteran Communist and former district head in charge of several communes, he had been removed from his official position by a central government work team that discovered in the course of a famine inspection that some 300 people had starved to death in his district in 1961. As for the other three Dachuan-based managers, two took care of the temple's accounts, while the third, a skillful calligrapher, served as a watchman in residence after having overseen the temple's construction. One of the two accountants had been the principal of a primary school until he was fired and branded a counterrevolutionary in 1954. The other accountant had been a "model chef," who cooked for county officials in the 1960's and still maintained good connections with people in the county government.

These men's divergent political backgrounds and social experiences might have impeded cooperation on many other projects. But when it came to temple management, these differences proved beneficial, for they could draw on one another's experiences and connections. Although they debated many issues among themselves, they firmly agreed that the welfare of the temple was paramount. This meant they would have to share not only responsibilities but memories as well, so they could present the public with a coherent explanation of the temple's historical and contemporary significance.

To achieve such interpretive unity, these temple managers rehearsed their accounts of the temple's past much as if performers preparing for a play. For instance, in order to solicit money for the construction work, they were first obliged to review the temple's history to make clear its former importance. To do this, they examined surviving genealogies and other old records. In the genealogy compiled in 1905, they found a document registering the number of sacrificial sheep received by the temple in the sixteenth century. Other local written records and orally transmitted memories allowed them to confirm the temple's destruction in 1785, its reconstruction in 1792, the circumstances under which it was burned down in 1864, who led its reconstruction in 1934, the confiscation of its land in 1953, its closure in 1958 by government decree, and, finally, its destruction in the 1974 Campaign Against Lin Biao and Confucius.

In reviewing the precarious history of this architectural landmark, the temple managers were keenly reminded of their community's troubled past. The political complications of their enterprise were brought home to them when they started to recover objects once owned by the temple. These fell into three categories: ritual objects, ordinary furniture, and building materials. The ritual objects included a large iron bell, incense burners, offering tables, and small lamps. These items had fallen into private hands in 1953, when the temple land was lost to land-reform activists and, above all, when those in charge of the temple became too intimidated to maintain tight control over this sacred site. The furniture included the primary school's desks and chairs. Some of these became office furnishings for the eight production teams set up in Dachuan in 1958. The building materials included bricks, tiles, stones, beams, windows, and gates. Stored in the village's carpenter's workshop after the temple's destruction in 1974, they were distributed to individual households when Dachuan's collectively held property was privatized in 1981.

To track down these remnants of the old temple, the temple managers had to question village leaders who had been in charge of Dachuan from the time of land reform to the early 1980's. In the process, they effectively placed the entire history of radical socialism under review. Former village cadres were asked who became the beneficiaries of the temple property and why. Since the building materials were the most important items to retrieve, the circumstances under which the old temple was torn down were thoroughly examined. Account books of the former "production brigade" and its eight subordinate "production teams" were checked. Witnesses were consulted, an itemized list of temple properties was drawn up, and a notice posted calling on individuals to return the temple's belongings voluntarily. In the end, over half the building materials used in the construction of the new Confucius temple came from the old temple's retrieved property.

In their efforts to reconstruct the temple's history and recover its belongings, the temple managers were inevitably exposed to many graphic details related to the temple's fate since the Com-

munist victory of 1949. This information made them extremely
nervous, for it enabled them to see their enterprise through a
lens of history focused on revolutionary campaigns marked by
arrests, imprisonment, and executions. They also began to realize, they said, that they had to find ways to convince government
and Party authorities that the reconstruction of the temple did
not represent the restoration of an illicit, superstitious cult. In
particular, they said, they emphasized the cultural legacy of
Confucius to assure officials in charge of the county's public security and religious affairs that the temple was a center of historical education instead of a cover for organizing suspect activities.

These precautions were not ill-advised. The county government continued in the early 1990's to keep secret files on the
Kongs. In the county archives, personal dossiers and court verdicts were kept that contained information on three of the temple managers and more than 100 members of the Kong lineage in
Yongjing. These documents were filled with confessions, police
reports, notes from informers, and court records, all from the
Maoist era. Although they were not updated, they remained
a potential weapon against the Kongs should the government
choose to crack down on kinship and religious organizations.

The Political Basis of Cultural Invention

To protect themselves, the temple managers tried to create a
safe public image for their enterprise. Part of their attempt to
achieve this is manifested in the unusual arrangement of spirit
tablets described above. It is also seen in the name they chose
for the new temple.

The temple managers ruled out the term *kong miao* (Temple
of Master Kong) on the ground that, in Chinese, it might be interpreted as a place only for the Kongs. They also decided against
sheng ren dian, or "Hall of Saints," the term most local villagers
used for the temple. This decision was based on their knowledge
that the title of saint (*sheng ren*) did not apply to local ancestors,

whose spirit tablets were also installed in Dachuan's old Confucius temple. Instead, they decided to name the temple *da cheng dian*, Monumental Hall of Great Accomplishment. Although the temple managers maintained that this name dates to the earliest known history of the temple, it actually is a term that was permitted only for state-controlled memorial halls in pre-Communist China. In such halls, government officials decided whose spirit tablets would be enshrined along with that of Confucius (Shryock [1932] 1966; Watters 1879). Arguing that attendance at these official halls was not restricted to descendants, the managers of Dachuan's Confucius temple chose this name to create the impression that their new temple, like the state-backed halls of the past, would function as more than an ancestor hall. In their public presentations, they asserted that the Dachuan temple actually bore this name for centuries and that this tradition had to be upheld. They also said that the temple's neutral name would serve as an invitation to people who were not Kongs to venerate Confucius. But in reasoning thus, they created several disturbing problems for themselves.

One problem was the question of whether the temple's central building could still be called Monumental Hall of Great Accomplishment if it contained the spirit tablets of local ancestors who were descendants of Confucius. The managers conceded that both in the past and at the present, the Monumental Hall of Great Accomplishment in Qufu excluded the spirit tablets of the Yansheng dukes, the direct heirs of Confucius living in the sage's hometown. At least in the Republican period (1911–49), these spirit tablets were installed in a group of memorial halls in the residence of the Yansheng Duke, a large compound near but distinct from Qufu's Confucius temple.

Sensitive to possible criticism of their ritual knowledge, the temple managers declared that as funds permitted, a side or rear hall would be built to enshrine the tablets for local ancestors separately. But this plan left yet another problem unsolved. When the temple managers added the tablets of Confucius's disciples to the temple, they announced that these historic person-

ages could be venerated as culture heroes and even as distant
ancestors by Dachuan residents who were not surnamed Kong
and by anyone from nearby villages. They bolstered this assertion by reasoning that the non-Kong villagers in Dachuan or residents of other nearby villages could be related to Confucius's disciples—because the latter bear more than 70 different surnames.
Since most Chinese and certainly the local villagers know little
about the Confucian pantheon, the temple managers hoped their
claim would go unchallenged.

Yet another problem: How could ritual unity be safeguarded
when the Kongs would have to kowtow to all the tablets while
worshippers not surnamed Kong could kowtow only to the tablets for Confucius and his disciples? To resolve this dilemma,
in 1991 the temple managers designed new ceremonial regulations.

Since 1985, Dachuan's ceremony honoring Confucius had
been held on the twenty-seventh day of the eighth month of the
Chinese lunar calendar, supposedly the sage's birthday. This
would begin with a procession on the late afternoon of the
twenty-sixth day to transport sacrificial offerings from the
slaughter site to the provisional shrine. The ceremony would
not begin until midnight.

After construction on the new temple was completed in 1991,
different ritual guidelines were developed. Under the new regulations, a midday ceremony was added, involving ordinary
members of the Kong lineage, affinal relatives, women and children from the Kong households, and even total strangers from
other villages and nearby factories. These people would be encouraged to pay their respects, by bows and kowtows, to the
spirit tablets of Confucius, the four acclaimed scholars of Confucianism, and the "seventy-two sagely disciples"—but not to the
Kong ancestors.

As for the midnight ceremony, its attendance would be restricted to selected representatives of the Kong lineage. These
people would play carefully defined roles, ranging from master
of ceremonies to musician and security guard. They would kow-

tow to all the tablets in the temple. Women born as Kongs or married to Kongs were allowed to attend the midnight ceremony but were excluded from such important rituals as offering sacrificial foods and reading elegiac texts in front of the enshrined tablets. At the end of the midnight liturgy, two men would stay behind the temple's closed gates to eat a portion of the sacrificial meat. To symbolize the continuity of bloodline, one of the men would be a representative of the most senior generation and the other would be chosen from the most junior generation of adults.

The success of the newly invented midday ceremony can be seen in an account book from the 1991 celebration. It records donations from fifteen of the sixteen non-Kong surname groups in Dachuan, whose representatives attended the midday ceremony. These donations were itemized as cash, lamp oil, paper flowers, colorful flags, and red banners with phrases of homage to Confucius. One non-Kong group, not recorded in the account book, had made a donation earlier. In return, the non-Kong participants in the daytime ritual received candies, peanuts, steamed bread, and fresh fruit. Only small slices of meat were given to participants, especially children. The sacrificial meat was reserved for a banquet to entertain the male elders from other Kong villages.

By maintaining the midnight ceremony, the temple managers sustained the temple's core function as a center for ancestor worship. And by creating a daytime ceremony, they inventively expanded its range of services. Most important, the double liturgy provided a much-needed shield against political complications. Reflecting on the past, the temple managers found it necessary to convince government officials that the temple was a public site for cultural education rather than exclusively an ancestor hall. In this respect, their inventive use of history and ritual is a classic case of political manipulation, raising interesting questions about the relation between collective memory, the institutional basis of recall, and the logic of cultural invention.

The precautions taken by the temple managers unmistakably bear the marks of cultural invention and political manipulation.

These people could not help but weigh their enterprise against the persecutions that had been suffered by the village's landlords and other community leaders. Having selected and reassembled important fragments of the past from genealogical records, oral tradition, and eye-witness accounts, they held special meetings to formulate ideas on ritual propriety, to reconstruct the temple's history, to step up fund-raising, and to select terms for the temple and its associated activities. This was a rehearsallike process that provided the foundation for a new configuration of individual memories by reorganizing personal recollections within the framework of group consultations, collective interests, and institutional responsibilities.

From a cross-cultural point of view (see, e.g., K. Baker 1990: 31–58; Bodnar 1989: 1201–21; Schwartz 1982: 374–97), this interplay of individual memory and memorial rehearsal poses a special problem for those who seek to measure the weight of history by looking only at its instrumentality. As noted at the beginning of this chapter, the tendency to treat cultural traditions as invented rather than historical realities has become fashionable in the recent work of anthropologists and social historians. Using this approach, scholars have highlighted the fabricated dimension of popular notions of the past. Nevertheless, an attempt to establish legitimacy by inventing tradition is hardly a random or arbitrary endeavor. Whatever is invented must be adjusted to meet various social considerations and cultural conventions. Most of all, the invention must also have an emotional appeal for the general public if it is to be at all viable. This last point will be amplified in the next chapter, which explores some highly emotional aspects of Dachuan's Confucius temple.

4

Memory of Communal Trauma

The Great Flood

At 10 A.M. on March 31, 1961, the Yanguoxia dam's floodgate was lowered. When it was lifted again, 48 hours later, water filled the reservoir behind the dam. To clear the land for this man-made lake, which covered 160 square kilometers, 16 villages were flooded and 9,014 people evicted. In all, 1,507 houses, 1,984 acres of farmland, 2,079 graves, and 110,975 fruit trees were lost.

The largest of the flooded villages was Dachuan. Nearly half its residents—1,298 people—were transferred to other places. Those who managed to stay behind—1,344 men, women, and children—moved to an elevated section of the old settlement and into a row of cemeteries at the foot of a barren hill behind the village. Having lost their most fertile farmland, abutting the northern bank of the Yellow River, the remaining population of Dachuan faced dangerous shortages of food, shelter, and medicine. A major famine already had taken its toll on this part of Gansu in late 1959, and China was still in the grip of "the three hard years" that followed the onset of the Great Leap Forward. By the time the dam began operating, the people of Dachuan were reduced to eating "substitute foodstuffs" (*dai shi pin*).

These were chaff, grass, wild herbs, elm bark, potato stems, fennel seeds, and even wall plaster. The famine, made worse by resettlement and the flooding of farmlands and orchards, claimed at least 50 lives in Dachuan.

Relocation drastically undermined the Kongs' sense of identity. Having experienced a series of brutal political campaigns, they were, in one blow, deprived of the land settled by their forebears in the early sixteenth century. Even with the passage of three decades, elderly men and women were visibly distraught as they described the disappearance of their old village. This experience remained as vivid as what psychologists call "flash-bulb memory"—an unforgettable experience formed during a high level of surprise and emotional response (see G. Cohen 1989: 128–130; Reber 1985: 430). The present chapter looks at how the experience of resettlement has been remembered in relation to Dachuan's Confucius temple.

Hydraulic Projects and Central Planning

Anthropologists who have studied large-scale hydraulic projects in developing countries attest that mandatory resettlement inevitably produces "a dehumanizing effect" (Farmer 1992: 19) and often results in "a crisis of cultural identity" (Scudder 1973: 51). What a dam or reservoir takes away from those it displaces is their moral map, the basis of their livelihood, and a historical touchstone of deeply emotional identities. Once resettled, the local population is forced to struggle with the shock of community breakup, the loss of farmland, the production of food in a radically different ecosystem, or the difficulty of adjusting to an alien habitat's social order (Ackerman 1973). All of these problems are starkly evident not only in the Dachuan case but in other Chinese river-basin development projects.

Large-scale reservoirs to generate electricity are an established feature of central planning in the People's Republic (Greer 1979; Jing 1989: 41–46; Smil 1984: 10–61, 1993: 99–116; Tian & Lin 1986: 185–229). When the Communist Party came to power in 1949, there were few reservoirs with a capacity exceeding 100,000,000 cubic meters; today China has more than 360 of them (State Statistics Bureau 1993b: 351). Most of these reservoirs were built during the 1960's and 1970's, when the Chinese government showed little concern for how or even whether the resettled villagers could cope with the breakup of community and lost livelihood. This indifference to individual and community needs was exemplified by the meager compensation offered to the relocatees. Sometimes, compensation was inadequate even to cover the cost of building temporary shelter or drinking water facilities. The problem of inadequate compensation was especially striking in Yongjing county.

Yongjing, surrounded by desolate and windswept hills, suffers all the physical constraints associated with the windswept loess plateau (World Bank 1988). In its heartland, however, the irrigation of arable fields is made possible by the Tao, Xia, and Yellow rivers descending from the highlands in Qinghai and Tibet. These three major rivers merge into one in Yongjing and must pass through extremely narrow gorges at Liujiaxia, Yanguoxia, and Bapanxia. These gorges provide an ideal setting for building a staircase of dams.

On July 30, 1955, Vice Premier Deng Zihui declared at a session of the National People's Congress that the government was planning to build 46 dams to "permanently control the Yellow River and tap its water resources." These dams, it was hoped, would end flooding, extend irrigation to 65 percent of the Yellow River valley, and produce an annual electric output of 110 billion kilowatt hours—ten times the nation's total output in 1954 (Deng 1955: 32–34).

In keeping with this ambitious plan, three large hydropower stations were built in Yongjing, at the Liujiaxia, Yanguoxia, and Bapanxia gorges. After construction began in 1958, the Yanguoxia Hydropower Station was built and its 57-meter-high dam activated in 1961. The Liujiaxia Hydropower Station, also begun in 1958, was completed in 1969. With its 147-meter-high dam and a vast reservoir, it was the largest of China's hydropower facilities until the early 1980's. Construction on the Bapanxia Hydropower Station started in 1968 and was completed in 1975. The communities around this station were under the jurisdiction of Lanzhou, but its reservoir behind a 33-meter-high dam flooded part of Yongjing.

These projects displaced 43,829 people and inundated 118,229 *mu* of farmland. Although they also caused a wave of resettlement in three other nearby rural counties, most of the relocated people were from Yongjing (Gansu Economic Planning Commission 1987). Within seventeen years (1958–75), a quarter of Yongjing's population was forcibly resettled. If there is a single event in this county's history that every adult in the valley area remembers, it is how thousands of people were forced to leave their native villages.

In most cases, the people of Yongjing opposed the relocation and put up various forms of resistance (Jing 1989: 41–46; Wang 1989: 6–7). The resistance was crushed, and many villagers were forced out of their homes by militiamen recruited from villages unaffected by the water projects. Most of the evicted villagers were resettled within Yongjing, on loess hills and the slopes above the submerged valley communities. Their chances of recovery after relocation were shattered by the flawed compensation policy. During the construction of the Yanguoxia project, the average per capita resettlement compensation was 250 yuan; those who were relocated because of the Liujiaxia project were supposed to receive an average of 364 yuan per person. In each case, the villagers received about 20 percent less than had been promised because of budget cuts. Those displaced by the Bapanxia project received an average of 1,100 yuan per head, which reflected a comparatively generous policy of compensation in the early 1970's. It enabled the resettlers to construct new houses with salvaged building materials. But even in this case, compensation was far too little to make up for the loss of farmland.[1] As for the compensation in the Yanguoxia and Liujiaxia projects, completed in 1961 and 1969, it amounted to outright robbery; what the government had offered would not even cover the lost fruit trees.

The grossly inadequate compensation helps to explain why the resettled villagers spent so many years trying to pull themselves out of penury. In 1988, the per capita income and availability of food among the displaced people were 30 percent lower than before the resettlement. The chief reason for these declines was the loss of farmland. Per capita access to farmland before resettlement was 2.72 *mu*; in 1988 it was 1.39 *mu* (Gansu Hydraulic Society 1988: 19). The latter amount, much of which consisted of newly cultivated land on loess hills, was not enough to provide food for one adult. In 1989, when I first worked in Yongjing, nearly half the displaced villagers were reported by the county government as being dependent on emergency food supplies and poverty-relief loans to avoid starvation.

A Master Narrative

The intense and persistent problems arising from the resettlement in Yongjing have never been publicly acknowledged by the Chinese government. Instead, it has created what might be described as a "master narrative." By that I mean a prototypical and consistent theme in the official accounts of the three water projects in Yongjing. Through propaganda, schools, and the news media, these projects have been glorified for their contributions to central planning, industrial growth, power generation, and general development of river valleys. By contrast, the official accounts have pointedly ignored the suffering of tens of thousands of relocated villagers. Two examples of the official narrative are a documentary film and a school textbook.

The film, produced by the Gansu Province Television Station, describes the Yanguoxia Hydropower Station as "the first glittering diamond" on the Yellow River. "Built in the shortest time and at the lowest cost," the narrator says, it occupies "a special chapter in China's socialist construction and industrial development."

As for the textbook, a story is told through the eyes of a child who accompanied his father on a tour of the Liujiaxia Hydropower Station, the largest of the three projects in Yongjing. From a distance, the child sees "a river-blocking dam as high as a 40-story building." After describing the breathtaking views from the top of the dam, the child says: "We took an elevator all the way down to the station's heart—the powerhouse. Inside, there was a neat line of five generators painted in green. Father told me that these five generators produce more electricity each year than was generated annually in the whole country before Liberation!" (People's Education Press [1988] 1991: 76–78). By invoking "Liberation," that is, the founding of the People's Republic in 1949, this story portrays the Liujiaxia project as one of the Communist regime's greatest accomplishments in hydraulic engineering.

In a calculated way, the master narrative created by the party-state legitimizes a brutal event by keeping a painful experience out of newspaper accounts, visual records, and other documents accessible to the public. As a typical exercise in organized amnesia, the viewing audience for the film that was televised on August 17, 1992, included the people of Dachuan. The textbook was compiled by an education office in Beijing and mandated for use at primary schools across China, including Yongjing, where the schoolchildren's parents or grandparents had been evicted because of the Liujiaxia project.

Disbelief and Destruction

How do the resettled villagers such as those in Dachuan regard these hydraulic projects? In many interviews, informants complained that they had been given little time to prepare for resettlement. They described the flood as if they had never expected it and recalled the loss of their village in cataclysmic terms. One villager said he had been among those who left the settlement at the last possible moment. "As I fled the village, the water was already up to my knees. I did not know how to swim. So I ran and ran, and never looked back until I reached the hillside." An elderly woman, then a young mother of three children, said that the rammed-earth walls of her house "broke apart and collapsed like a stack of cards." Another villager, only twelve when Dachuan was flooded, said he would never forget his grandmother's wailing. "My family escaped to a graveyard, a higher place for shelter, and I fell asleep there. Then I woke up. And there was Grandma, kneeling on the ground and crying at the top of her voice. I looked downward for our home in the village and could see nothing but water."

Listening to such emotional accounts about the flooding of the village, I initially assumed, wrongly, that the government had opened the floodgate without warning. Eventually I came to realize that the situation was far more complicated. It was on September 27, 1958, that the Yanguoxia project was inaugurated, following a mass rally at which authorities from the central and provincial governments heralded this project as a national showcase for the Great Leap Forward. A resettlement committee was immediately set up in the nearby city of Linxia, which included government officials and construction managers. One of the first decrees the resettlement committee issued was addressed to local cadres responsible for villages located below the water level of the planned reservoir. In this order, the cadres were told to publicize the project's economic and political significance. A month later, more detailed orders concerning resettlement were issued.[2] To estimate expected property losses, the committee organized a team of officials to conduct a village-by-village inspection. The inspectors were asked to do two things: to urge villagers to prepare for a timely departure and to make an inventory of personal property and collective farmland.

The resettlement committee's task was grossly misunderstood by the local villagers. At first, government officials and construction managers boasted that the Yellow River could be dammed within a year. But many villagers, especially the older ones, scoffed at the official proclamation. Children were told by their elders that in the 1940's the Nationalist government had failed to build a dam in this area despite technical assistance from the United States. The anecdote referred to a team of Chinese and American hydraulic specialists who had visited Yongjing in September 1945. They were led by Zhang Guangdou, head of the Nationalist government's Hydropower Commission, and John Savage, chief engineer of the Grand Coulee Dam in Washington state. After Zhang and Savage selected a dam site in Yongjing, they drafted a feasibility study (Yongjing County Gazetteer Committee 1992, vol. 16). The study was shelved when the civil war between Communists and Nationalists intensified. This previous failure to harness the Yellow River gave rise to the widespread assumption that the Communist-led dam project would meet a similar fate.

The villagers also misjudged the intent of the inspectors sent down by the resettlement committee. Back in late 1956, the majority of villagers in Yongjing county had joined so-called high-level cooperatives. These were collective units of production, but the villagers were still allowed to keep a small number of cultivated fields and draft animals for private use. In October 1958, only a month after the dam project was started at Yanguoxia, the 154 "high-level cooperatives" that had been already formed in Yongjing were placed under the unified leadership of people's communes. With the founding of these communes, the cultivated fields and draft animals still in private hands were collectivized. The only major private possessions left to the local people were houses, furniture, domestic animals, and those fruit trees inside residential compounds. Villagers feared, however, that even these private possessions would be seized by goverment officials to expand the economic basis of the newly established communes. So when the officials from the resettlement committee began their village-by-village inspections and set up registration desks in community squares to record landed and movable properties, the local residents suspected that their real intention was to step up the collectivization drive by first registering and then abolishing whatever private possessions remained. Instead of reporting to the inspectors the actual number and value of their possessions, the villagers greatly understated them.

This response was also related to the impact of an earlier political movement, namely, the Communist-led land reform. During land reform, the local population had been classified into five classes—landlords, rich, middle, lower-middle, and poor peasants—primarily by the per capita farmland available to a given household. After the landlords and rich peasants were humiliated at public rallies and deprived of much of their property, they were stigmatized and subjected to constant persecution by local cadres. So when officials from the resettlement committee tried to estimate the possessions of households below the reservoir's planned water line, the villagers feared that the information was being collected not only for another round of expropriations, but also for an adjustment of class labels.

To avoid the possibility of falling into a bad class category, villagers in Dachuan resorted to various methods of deliberately undervaluing their property. One villager recalled: "My father told me that another land reform was under way. He took down wall paintings, dismantled carved window-frames, and hid cast-iron door handles so as to make our house look cheap. Actually, the rooms had been built only five years before, but he told the inspection team that the rooms were twenty years old."

Once the Yanguoxia dam was finally built, the villagers panicked at the realization that they had misread the government's purpose. Still, despite the news that embankments for the dam's reservoir were also nearly complete, few families left Dachuan. Most people refused to go, believing that the dam would not be activated as long as they stayed in the valley. This further delayed preparations for resettlement and resulted in the government's deployment of militia to evict the villagers.

Around the time of the Chinese lunar New Year in 1961, which began on February 15 that year, most people had been forced to move from Dachuan into other communities or temporary shelters on higher ground. But building materials still needed to be transported to the new settlements, and to guard these materials from being stolen or taken by mistake, an unknown number of people stayed behind until the dam's floodgate was lowered. They were rescued by relatives or fled on their own as the water flooded the streets.

A Vanished World?

A higher section of Dachuan was not immediately affected by the reservoir, but eventually it, too, had to be abandoned because the groundwater was forced up to the land's surface when silt accumulating in the reservoir blocked off natural aquifers. Gradually, even the highest part of Dachuan's original settlement was overtaken by the reservoir, as swamps formed and marshy fields were converted into fish ponds.

In physical terms, the old site of Dachuan has been erased, but it continues to be "seen" in a cultural sense. During a boat trip I took in 1989, a young man waved a stick at an island-like mound in the reservoir and said that it was where the village's finest farmland once lay. He then pointed toward his feet and explained that we were directly above the entrance to the former village's main street. Though nothing could be seen through the deep, murky water, he directed the boatman to sail along this invisible street. He singled out a spot in the reservoir and said that was the site of his father's homestead. It was his grandparents, he said, who had told him these things. When asked whether life in the past was any better than today, he responded with a look as if an utterly moronic question had been raised. Of course the past was better, he answered, describing the many date trees and water wheels, and the high quality of farmland, the village had once enjoyed.

This vision of an idyllic past is a result of education by an older generation who lead their young people in a backward journey through time. Because of rapid population growth, at least half the present population in Dachuan was not even born or was too young to remember anything about how the reservoir was built. Given these demographics, cross-generational memory gives children a sense of their origin and notions of local history.

And when they are told that their lost village was once a wonderful place to live, they begin to share an older generation's conviction of having been terribly wronged.

During formal interviews, casual conversations, and drinking parties from 1989 to 1993, informants in Dachuan spent much time describing for me the fertility of the lost farmland, the familiar scenes in the old streets, the threshing grounds where they played games as children, or where the sweetest dates were grown. Like the young man in the boat, even villagers who had been born years after the resettlement spoke with great nostalgia of the places where their parents or grandparents once lived. In group interviews in particular, the informants corrected inaccuracies in one another's accounts and discussed many matters in impressive detail, reciting the exact number of trees or the precise amount of land that Dachuan had lost. By contrast, they rarely volunteered any information about what had happened to their ancestors' tombs.

The Fate of Family Tombs

Before the village was flooded, the Kongs managed to retrieve the remains of their parents, grandparents, and great-grandparents. But most tombs from earlier generations were deserted in the rush to relocate. To protect the quality of the water in the reservoir, construction workers cleared out human remains from the older tombs and literally tossed them together with tons of human waste and animal manure at dumping sites above the reservoir. Unlike many other aspects of the relocation, the fate of the family tombs was a difficult subject to explore in interviews. Hidden away in the recesses of private thought, feelings about the ancestors' fate were extremely hard to articulate. The loss of ancestors' remains was considered both a communal and a personal failure, and any references to it tended to provoke profound pain.

At the heart of this distressing matter is what Lawrence Langer (1991) has described as "inappropriate guilt," that is, blaming the self for what might in fact have been unavoidable. Put another way, the Kongs, especially the elderly men, were burdened by the thought that perhaps they could have done something to prevent the loss of so many tombs. But this judgment was shaped by afterthoughts rather than growing out of a situation over which they had little control.

It helps to repeat that the Kongs in this area trace their ancestry to Confucius through four brothers. Dachuan was chosen by the four brothers' father because of its favorable geomancy: The village site was in an S-shaped river valley, which to him symbolized a flying phoenix, and was in front of a mountain range whose structure resembled, to his eyes, the writhing shape of a dragon. With these auspicious signs, the father decided on this place for his sons' new home.

The tomb of the eldest of the four brothers was immediately submerged by the reservoir. The tombs of the second and third brothers were flattened when cemeteries on higher ground had to be converted into farmland and residential areas after much of the village was submerged. The tomb of the fourth brother fell victim to a state-owned fertilizer plant, which was built near Dachuan in the mid-1960's to take advantage of the reservoir's water supply and the cheap energy from the hydroelectric station. For various reasons, no concerted effort was made to protect these important tombs, but perhaps the most crucial reason is that the organizational structure of the Kong lineage had been too ravaged by previous political campaigns to allow the Kongs to unite at a time of crisis or to negotiate with managers of the fertilizer plant to save the last of these tombs.[3]

According to a government document I copied at the county archives, Dachuan lost a total of 209 tombs. They clearly had been opened by construction workers, because a footnote to this document states that the reservoir's bottom was "thoroughly cleansed for sanitation purposes," and that workers removed "twenty tons of garbage, human waste, and material detrimental to people's health." The detrimental material is a euphemism for the bones cleared from tombs before the reservoir was filled.

At a small drinking party where I showed three elderly men

this document, they said that the official figure of 209 represents only the tombs below the reservoir's water line. It does not include tombs on higher ground, which, they reluctantly explained, were demolished when villagers were forced uphill and had to construct shelters and cultivate new fields on what had been cemeteries. At the end of the drinking party, one of the three elderly villagers confided that the street corner where I often played Chinese chess (xiang qi) with neighbors of my host family was the site of a former graveyard. Pressed for more information, he identified other sites in the village that were built over graveyards.

In the words of the elderly man who hesitantly spoke of the geomancy of the village's present-day location, "the houses of the dead (yin zhai) and the houses of the living (yang zhai) are terrifyingly close." The overlapping of the world of the dead and the world of the living violates a basic principle of Chinese geomancy (Feuchtwang 1974; Freedman 1966: 5–15). Worst of all, the village's streets and residential houses are built over desecrated tombs, some of which were directly destroyed by the villagers themselves. Younger people, who are somewhat less disturbed by their village's unfavorable geomancy, said that it was not uncommon to uncover human bones when they dug out cellars to store their vegetables over the winter.

Ancestral Remains Relocated

Although the older tombs were abandoned, the remains of immediate ancestors were collected and reburied. Such tasks should properly have been performed by corpse-handlers, who would be given food and wine as payment. As in a Cantonese community studied by James Watson (1988: 75–111), such people were male, poor, and marginal members of society. The difference in the Dachuan case is that the corpse-handlers were local residents. But in the haste of relocation, even these people were busy removing their own ancestors or dealing with other pressing matters.

One tradition after another was violated: The bones were

placed not in miniature coffins, but in paper bags for cement; the locations of the new tombs were chosen haphazardly, with scant regard for geomancy; reburials were conducted without proper rituals. Such was the villagers' state of shock that numbness supplanted customary lamentations of mourning.

When asked how he gathered the ancestral bones, an old man looked disconcerted. Then, as if accused of having committed a grave mistake, he grumbled: "We just picked up the bones with chopsticks and put them into cement bags we collected from the reservoir construction sites. We carried the bones on our backs and buried them in Quannian Mountain. I tell you it was no time for being proper about such things."

A seventy-four-year-old man made an obvious effort to remember whether any reburial ceremonies were conducted, but after a few moments he shook his head: "How could anyone hold ceremonies? We knew the dead were tormented by the living, but nobody could get meat or any food to make sacrifices to comfort the deceased. At that time, food was rationed and kept at the big collective dining halls. You cannot imagine how we were starving. Even the living had to eat grass roots."

Another elderly villager explained that at the time of relocation he and two of his brothers were the most senior among their great-grandfather's descendants. Before the reservoir was filled, he and his brothers worked together to rebury the remains of their parents, grandfather, and great-grandfather. They supervised the reburial of their father's brother and their grandfather's brother. They saw to it that the bones of their late brothers were moved, by the brothers' children. "In two days," he said, "we relocated ten tombs and ate nothing. We had no appetite. We were too tired, too anxious. We looked like ghosts climbing out of graves."

The haste with which so many tombs were moved can be detected in the size of the new graves. For instance, I noticed in the mountain behind the village a graveyard on a small terrace. At first, it looked like a communal burial ground for children. Aside from a few normal-sized tombs toward the front, most of the graves were very small, each occupying less than half a square meter. They were also surprisingly low. When the village's accountant and the Confucius temple watchman were asked about these small tombs, they first said that dead children are customarily cremated and thus have no tombs. The small graves I had seen contained the reburied remains. Because they were dug shallow and no extra earth was added to compress them, they were low and small to begin with. Several of these graves, I was told, contained more than one person's bones because a single box or paper sack was sometimes used to collect remains from several tombs. Despite efforts to carry the bones in boxes within a larger box or to separate different layers of bones in a sack with paper or cloth, some remains were mixed together, a serious violation of the Chinese notion that an ancestor's remains must be kept intact.

Even though the Kongs tried their best to save the remains of immediate ancestors, some were too weak from hunger or too pressed to flee to open tombs, remove bones, and carry them uphill. In such cases, they wrote the names of the dead on wooden sticks and buried these on higher ground as though they were actual remains. To be blunt, some of the "reburial graves" are a sham, in the sense that they hold neither bones nor coffins —another aspect of the relocation the Kongs were reluctant to discuss.[4]

The Possibility of Redemption

Anthropologists studying China may feel uncomfortable with the concepts of guilt and redemption entering into analyses of ethnographic or historical data collected from Chinese communities. One reason for their uneasiness is that these concepts can be very problematic in cultural translation. While we might approximate the English term "guilt" with that of "internal shame," or *nei jiu* in Chinese, it is more difficult to find an equivalent for "redemption." And even if the Chinese term *shu zui*, or "atoning for one's crime," is accepted to mean "redemption," to follow the usual translation offered by dictionaries, it should be recognized that the Chinese term has a Buddhist origin, referring to deliverance from suffering as well as expiation for a sin, misdeed, or crime.

But no matter how difficult, cultural translation is what anthropologists do. And during fieldwork, I noticed local informants using a variety of local words and phrases that could reflect notions of guilt. For example, a privately expressed fear among some Kongs is that ancestors were profoundly disturbed by the makeshift reburials. This was described as a "shock to the ancestors," a "great affront," and a "deep disgrace." The elderly Kongs in particular found it hard to make peace with themselves on this matter, as reflected in their avoidance of the subject. Even a number of older villagers who came to know me quite well confined their remarks to a collective frame of reference. They were reluctant to refer directly to how they themselves picked up ancestral bones or how their brothers reacted to the loss of older graves. Their emphasis was on how every family reburied ancestors in the same way and why all the families failed to preserve the older tombs.

It should be added that the Kongs avoided talking about their ancestral tombs and remains not only in the presence of outsiders but among themselves, especially when children were around. This evasion, among other things, operated as a defense against painful memories of individual failure. The sense of failure over the loss of older tombs and the lack of proper reburials for immediate ancestors has been joined by apprehension, because villagers and domestic animals are now living above desecrated graves and defiled cemeteries. The frequent discovery of human bones when ground is dug to build underground storage areas reminds the villagers that they are living above a ruined abode of the dead. This disturbing association complicates any potential memorial evocation of the relocation and its connection to family tombs.

Tainted by self-blame and by fear of inauspicious geomancy, memories of what happened to tombs and remains are understandably stored away in the recesses of private thought and internal mourning. This does not mean, however, that private memories regarding the ancestral tombs are altogether sealed off from public discourse. Although borne by individuals, the power of such hidden memories has been felt in public arenas on certain occasions. One of these was the reconstruction of the Confucius temple. After seven years of preparation, sufficient funds were raised to build the temple. It was built only three months after a piece of land was found in the already crowded village.

The temple's reconstruction may have provided a certain redemption. Its central hall is not only larger, cleaner, and busier than the provisional shrine, but is considered far holier thanks to a series of consecration rituals. These included a site-finding ceremony performed by two geomancers, a ritual to install the building's cross-beam, a solemn liturgy to accompany the inscribing of the soul tablets, and special services to receive major donations. Through this process of consecration, the temple offers the Kongs a proper place to commemorate the ancestors whose tombs were lost either directly to the reservoir or as a result of the villagers' confusion and inability to salvage them.

Most important, the temple provides a public memorial to the forced resettlement. Flanking the entrance of the temple's central hall are two placards notable for their great size and fine calligraphy. The one on the left lists the households that contributed money for the temple's construction. It displays the names of 1,346 heads of Kong households from 25 villages, including two rural communities in Qinghai province that were settled long ago by Kongs from Dachuan. The placard on the right bears a memorial text reviewing the temple's history and its latest incarnation. In the recent wave of temple construction in this part of rural China, a common practice has been to inscribe a memorial text on a large placard for the new temple, usually extolling those who headed the construction project. This format is followed in the memorial text at Dachuan's Confucius temple.

Written in black ink and prominently displayed, the rebuilt temple's memorial text begins with a tribute to Confucius's prestige in Chinese culture and traces the history of the old temple, with references to its original location, its decline, and its destruction. It then reviews how the new temple was constructed, lists the temple managers, and explains how cash and material contributions to the temple project were used. Within this rather lengthy text, the temple's fate in the past few decades is summarized in a single sentence: "Damaged by the construction of the reservoir and destroyed in the Cultural Revolution, the Monumental Hall of Great Accomplishment suffered flooding, rotted in a salt marsh, and finally was dismantled during the Anti–Lin Biao and Confucius Campaign."

It is worth noting that this passage includes such concrete details as the reservoir, the flooding, and the salt marsh. This means that the immensely painful experience of resettlement has been inscribed into the public record and prominently displayed at precisely the place where the living communicate with the dead. The composition of this temple's memorial text was an institutional decision, the result of many discussions of what messages to include and how they could best be presented. In this sense, the inclusion of forced resettlement in the memorial text suggests that the temple is not only a religious symbol of redemption, but also a political manifesto of local protest against an ambitious and extremely disruptive project imposed from above.

1. The birthplace of Confucius, Qufu, Shandong province. This and the
two following photographs are taken from a bilingual guidebook, *Qufu,
the Native Place of Confucius* (Beijing, Cultural Relics Publishing
House, 1990).

2. Entrance to
the Yansheng
Duke's resi-
dence, Qufu.

3. The current Yansheng Duke and his family (photograph taken in the 1940's).

4. Dachuan village's Confucius temple, 1991. The carved unpainted wood is typical of the local architecture. *Jun Jing*

5. The temple managers in 1991, standing under a plaque inscribed "Monumental Hall of Great Accomplishment," the standard name for the central hall of a Confucius temple. *Jun Jing*

6. In 1992, a preschool was opened at Dachuan's Confucius temple. Here, the temple's watchman (right) assembles the village children and their teacher for a photograph. *Jun Jing*

7. A Kong family from the Gansu provincial capital, Lanzhou, visiting Dachuan on Confucius's birthday in 1992, to donate money and present a memorial plaque. *Jun Jing*

8. The plaque from the Lanzhou Kongs is carried to the Confucius temple in Dachuan. The inscription reads, "The benevolence of the ancestors is as vast as the sea." *Jeanne Moore*

9. After a ceremony marking Confucius's birth in Dachuan in 1992, blessed offerings were distributed among the celebrants. Here, a child is fed a slice of canned pear. *Jeanne Moore*

10. A Kong baby is dressed as his family prepares to attend the Confucius birthday celebration in Dachuan in 1991. *Jun Jing*

11. Sacrificial animals are blessed before being carried to the Confucius temple built in neighboring Xiaochuan in 1992. Here, the "Bright-Eyed" rabbit (front) is displayed alongside the "Clear-Voiced" rooster. *Jeanne Moore*

12. The Kong elders call on the ancestors to accept the offerings of food and drink and to bestow their blessings on the assembled. Xiaochuan, 1992. *Jeanne Moore*

13. Watching the procession wend its way through the streets were three elderly Kong women, all with bound feet, who had married out to other villages. Xiaochuan 1992. *Jeanne Moore*

14. The local schoolteachers worked closely with the Kong elders in organizing children, who waved bright-colored paper hoops, for the procession. Xiaochuan, 1992. *Jeanne Moore*

15. Along the procession route, villagers set up tables laden with refreshments and cigarettes to be offered to participants in the procession. Here, one of the honored guests leading the procession accepts a cup of clear spirits. Xiaochuan, 1992. *Jeanne Moore*

16. The procession transferring sacrifices reaches the outskirts of the village, near the Confucius temple. Xiaochuan, 1992. *Jeanne Moore*

17. As the procession approaches the temple grounds, women holding bundles of incense sticks fall to their knees. Xiaochuan, 1992. *Jeanne Moore*

18. At the public festival the morning after the consecration of the Confucius temple, three of the temple managers wear the bright-colored silk sashes presented to them by well-wishers. Xiaochuan, 1992. *Jeanne Moore*

5

~~~

Memory of Local Animosity

A Harvest of Bitterness

A notable characteristic of the Maoist campaigns that ravaged the Chinese countryside was the close link between political victims and their tormentors. Rural society was not a passive universe helplessly rocked by political campaigns launched from above. What the political campaigns did was to unlock a Pandora's box, pushing the local agents of the state into the hunt for concrete targets at the grassroots levels, in pursuit of the "perpetual revolution" envisioned by Mao (Chan, Madsen, & Unger 1984; 1992; Huang 1989; Madsen 1984; 1990: 175–98). At the center of thousands of villages were local collaborators trying to manipulate these campaigns to their own advantage. In many cases, they were motivated by long-standing hostility between individuals, families, or local factions. More often than not, their victims were neighbors, childhood playmates, or even immediate relatives by blood or marriage (see Crook & Crook 1959, 1979; Friedman, Pickowicz, & Selden 1991; Hinton 1966, 1983; Shue 1980; Vogel 1969: 27–62; C. K. Yang 1959).

In the late 1970's, with Mao's death and the end of the Cultural Revolution, Chinese society was beginning the process of recovery from national chaos and personal tragedy. By the late 1980's, the average citizen was enjoying a visibly greater degree of wealth and somewhat more individual freedom. Yet the social landscape has remained, as Richard Madsen put it, "littered with dangerous memories of arbitrary injuries" (1990: 187). This is especially the case in the countryside. Whereas urban residents now can secure a job transfer or change of residence to escape the company of old enemies, rural residents are less able to avoid face-to-face encounters with adversaries from the past. For most of them, their home villages are fixed places of work and domicile. It is extremely difficult to move one's entire family to another village. It is even more difficult to secure official permits for urban residence. Within the tightly defined physical and social boundaries of Chinese villages, the personal recollections of radical socialism, peopled by brutal oppressors, helpless victims, temporary allies, and loyal supporters, are provocative and tied to concrete incidents.

In a number of recent studies, the aftermath of economic reforms and sociopolitical changes in rural China has been addressed by scholars in terms of leadership transformation (Hartford 1985), new forms of social control (Huang 1989), population control (Greenhalgh 1993: 219–50), disparities in personal wealth (Yan 1992: 1–23), management of ritual and religious affairs (Anagnost 1987: 147–76; MacInnis 1989; Siu 1989b: 195–212, 1990: 765–94), the penetration of capitalism from Hong Kong (Potter & Potter 1990), and economic strategies of the family or community (Johnson 1993: 103–38; Ruf 1994). If any general agreement arises from these studies, it is that the end of collectivism profoundly altered the power structure of rural communities. It is within this context that this chapter uses the Dachuan case to explore the impact of memory on community politics. The focal point of the discussion is the struggle over village administration and ancestor worship.

Ancestor Worship and Power Struggle

Worship of ancestors in private homes and in the graveyards of individual households never really ceased in Dachuan, except during the early phase of the Cultural Revolution. But elaborate sacrificial rites involving Kongs from Dachuan and other Kong villages were suspended from 1950 on. They were resumed only in 1984, in a three-room carpenters' workshop. The chief organizer of the first ceremony at this provisional shrine was Dachuan's Party secretary. A land-reform activist and the village's undisputed ruler from 1958 to 1985, he was known locally as *lao shu ji*, or "old Party secretary." Other cadres, mostly his comrades-in-arms, helped raise money to cover the ritual expenses, and, together with the local Party boss, occupied the place of honor during the ritual proceedings.

The involvement of Dachuan's Party organization in the reinstitution of this ancestral rite was a calculated move. For many years, the Party secretary and his associates had worked as local accomplices in the crusades against what was characterized in the Chinese press as "feudal superstition." In addition, they actively participated in the Party's efforts to achieve thought reform and social control by informing on alleged troublemakers in the village. Some of their secret reports to government officials resulted in police detention, confessions extracted by beatings, and even lengthy imprisonment. Their role as local informers is evident in village files and in personal dossiers they compiled and sent to higher authorities. During my fieldwork, I examined some of these documents, which were filed in the Yongjing county archives.

For the Party secretary and his lieutenants still in power after decollectivization, setting up an ancestor shrine was part of the ideological shift of the post-Mao era, an opportunity to recapture influence. In a village riven with bad feelings and internal distrust caused by the resettlement and by successive political campaigns, ancestor worship provided a rare point of consensus. It furnished the village cadres with a unique form of social organization, which allowed them to accumulate what Arjun Appadurai has called "a sacred resource" (1981:201). To amass and control this resource by managing its ritual expressions—the ceremony and the ceremonial site—was to claim a meritorious service to the community and create a passage to moral authority. By definition, moral authority is the ability to lead by actions that are deemed ethically exemplary in a given culture. In a situation in which the administrative power of Dachuan's village cadres was rapidly shrinking, leadership in ancestor worship could be a key step toward winning respect, popularity, and even trust.

But these cadres, who had ruled Dachuan in the collective era and were still clinging to power in 1984, failed to establish lasting control over the provisional shrine. Within a year their administrative positions were taken over by younger villagers, and they consequently had to surrender control over ancestor worship to a group of elderly, classically educated Kongs, who formed an alliance with the new, younger village cadres. To understand this shift in the village's administrative and religious life, we need to consider what else was going on about this time—notably, the petition drives waged by the resettled villagers of Yongjing seeking further compensation from the central government for damages caused by the construction of the three dams and reservoirs. This grassroots movement was to reshape the power structure of Dachuan.

Memory, Protest, and Compensation

Before decollectivization, local resentment over the three hydraulic projects built by the central government in Yongjing did not give rise to public protests such as sit-ins or street demonstrations. The social and economic problems caused by these projects were handled by community efforts under the leadership of rural cadres. Decollectivization, which took place in Yongjing in 1981, returned agricultural production to a household basis. This provoked immediate unrest, which can be traced to the fate of two kinds of people, known as "pushed-backs" (*hou kao*) and "thrown-ins" (*cha hua*).

The "pushed-backs" were those who, in the course of reservoir-related resettlement, had retreated to the higher slopes or loess hills behind the residential sites of their former villages. During decollectivization, which caused a vicious round of property disputes between old neighbors and even close relatives, the "pushed-backs" were painfully reminded of how much farmland had been lost and how little land they would receive in the distribution of collective assets. The "thrown-ins" were people who had been transferred from their native villages to other communities. They also suffered in the redistribution of land. As outsiders who had long been discriminated against by native residents, they were at a disadvantage during decollectivization, which was accompanied by a fierce struggle for top-quality farmland, draft animals, fish ponds, production tools, and building materials, little of which they could claim had ever belonged to them.

Whether they had been pushed uphill or thrown in with other communities, the resettled villagers fared badly during decollectivization. This reinforced their conviction that all their problems could be traced to the reservoir resettlement. This feeling intensified as the rural economic reforms were increasingly glorified by the Chinese news media. The official propaganda drives that celebrated "get-rich-quick" individuals or "become-wealthy-first" villages in other parts of China had a dual effect upon the displaced villagers in Yongjing. It made them keenly aware of the rapidly widening regional disparities in personal wealth. And it intensified their belief that they deserved special treatment from the state since they had sacrificed so much for national development.

It is interesting that grievances erupted into public protests just as state authorities and local officials were trying to address some of the problems occasioned by resettlement. Faced with mounting complaints from the relocated villagers that they deserved cheap and unlimited use of electricity, Gansu provincial authorities asked the central government in 1981 to forgive debts incurred by the resettled villagers in using electricity for irrigation. The central government approved this request in 1982, and waived electricity bills totaling 1.35 million yuan

(Linxia Prefectural Government 1987: 6). To further pacify the resettled villagers, the central government allowed them to use electricity at a discounted price fixed for a term of ten years (Yongjing County Government 1987: 11). From 1985 to 1987, Yongjing was allowed by state authorities to extract, in the name of the resettled villagers, over ten million yuan from the Liujia-xia and Yanguoxia hydrostations (Linxia Prefectural Government 1987: 6). This money went to 30 local projects to upgrade irrigation facilities and alleviate soil erosion.

But the central government's concessions failed to soothe the relocated people in Yongjing, partly because no compensation was given directly to individuals and partly because the county government had mismanaged relief funds.[1] It was against this background that riots and other forms of public protest began breaking out. Taxes on crops grown along the reservoirs were widely evaded; illegal diversion of electricity became rampant; interest was not paid on loans from state-run banks; and state-run factories that had moved to Yongjing during the 1960's and 1970's were hit by sabotage during disputes with villages over the question of how to handle land acquisitions, water facilities, and industrial pollution. After a demonstration that included window-smashing, a government agency gave up its planned move into a new office building. It had been rumored that the building was constructed with poverty-relief funds allocated by the central government for the resettled villagers (Wang 1989: 20).

Organized petition drives took place every year from 1982 to 1992. Letters of complaint and appeals for financial aid were delivered to the township, county, prefectural, and provincial governments. Petition drives were sometimes timed to coincide with important national events. For instance, a group of villagers prepared to travel to Beijing as the Thirteenth National Congress of the Chinese Communist Party was about to convene in 1987 (Linxia Prefectural Government 1987: 5). Their aim was to deliver to the congress a handwritten plea, which included requests for low-interest loans and free supplies of irrigation equipment. Through the determined intervention of county and prefectural officials, the petitioners were finally persuaded to change their destination from Beijing to Lanzhou.

Petition Drives and Leadership Change

An examination of internally circulated reports filed by officials at the county, prefectural, and provincial levels suggests that the Kongs of Dachuan played a key role in nearly all major acts of defiance of state authority. Two Kongs from Dachuan even traveled to Beijing in 1985 to demand compensations. When they returned home empty-handed, they organized a sit-in at a township government office, which ended in a fistfight. One of the representatives who had gone to Beijing and organized the sit-in was arrested by police from the county government. In response to his arrest, a group of militant youths from Dachuan kidnapped the township's chief administrator and Party secretary and held them in a residential compound guarded by ferocious dogs. Then, some two hundred angry villagers marched on the county seat. They shouted their demands for justice in front of the county government compound and offered to free the township officials in exchange for the man from Dachuan. The "hostages" were indeed swapped with the approval of senior provincial officials, who did not want the demonstration to escalate into a broader protest.

This incident had repercussions that were to alter drastically Dachuan's power structure. Even before 1985, the position of the village's Party secretary and his associates was being challenged. About half of the 60 members of the village's Party organization had attained their Party membership while they were serving in the military, attending technical schools, working on state-organized construction projects, or holding junior-level government jobs outside the village. In other words, these people had joined the Party outside Dachuan, and upon returning to Dachuan, they found themselves excluded from the power circle dominated by the long-reigning Party secretary. Increasingly dissatisfied with this situation, these younger, ambitious, and well-traveled Party members drew on connections they had formed during their years outside the village to pressure the township Party committee to withdraw their support of Dachuan's Party secretary. Meanwhile, they campaigned among other village Party members to find a new leader, arguing that the incumbent Party secretary could not be trusted. As evidence, they cited Dachuan's repeated failures to secure adequate compensation for the reservoir resettlement of 1961.

When the township officials were kidnapped, the Party secretary of Dachuan declared to his superiors that he had nothing to do with it, which was true. But by distancing himself from this event, he undermined his position in his home village. When the village Party members finally convened to discuss Dachuan's future in the aftermath of the violent confrontations with the county and township officials, those who had been neutral or loyal to the Party secretary came under tremendous pressure from other villagers to support his removal from office. The names of two candidates, one for the position of Party secretary and the other for village head, were submitted to the township government in early 1986. Both nominees had worked behind the scenes in the demonstration and earlier petition drives. That their appointments were promptly approved by township officials was by no means accidental.

After the demonstration by the Kongs ended, three senior township officials were replaced, and the new township leaders were instructed by the county government to mollify the Kongs to avoid future trouble. The reshuffle in the township government was a well-thought-out move on the part of the county's senior officials. The three new township cadres all had close ties to Dachuan. Two were surnamed Kong; one lived in Dachuan and the other had been relocated from Dachuan in 1961. The third, the new head of the township government's Party committee, was surnamed Cui; his mother was a Kong from Dachuan. The county authorities who appointed these people were apparently aware of the utility of kinship in pacifying the Kongs. And these new township officials seemed to appreciate that problems with the Kongs in Dachuan could mar their own careers as bureaucrats. Under the jurisdiction of the township government were ten villages in which about half the inhabitants were surnamed Kong or related to the Kongs by marriage. Three of these villages were predominantly Kong settlements; one of them, which is named Zhongzhuang and within walking distance of Dachuan, was the seat of the township government. Dachuan is the largest of the ten villages and also the oldest Kong settlement in Yongjing. For the three newly appointed officials of the township government, winning over Dachuan would be a first step toward controlling all ten villages.

Village Politics and Temple Politics

After the new Party secretary and village head of Dachuan took office, they selected their assistants and imposed a fine on the old Party secretary's family for having violated the state's birth-control policy. Under normal circumstances, village cadres would protect one another and could use various means to dodge the population controls. But Dachuan's old Party secretary had been expelled from the local circle of protection. The penalty on his family was not a large sum, but it discredited him within the rural bureaucracy up to the county level and further undercut the power he had amassed since land reform.

Meanwhile, the former Party secretary's moral standing in Dachuan eroded under the weight of new rumors. In 1974, when the Confucius temple was dismantled and its components were hidden by village cadres to avoid confiscation by commune leaders, the Party secretary was in charge of distributing temple property to the various production teams. Gossip now had it that he had held back some of the temple material and transferred it to his close associates for private use. Having been defeated in local politics, fined for violating the birth-control policy, and hu-

miliated by stories suggesting he had embezzled temple property, he suffered a stroke and became bedridden. In 1989 he died,
his reputation ruined.

The installation of new leaders redirected the course of ancestor worship in Dachuan. The new village head took over the
management of the provisional ancestor shrine. Two years later,
in 1988, he left public office to become the foreman of a highly
profitable construction team. He employed forty to sixty workers, depending on the season, all recruited in Dachuan. In 1993,
he had an income in five figures and was said to be the third-
richest man in Dachuan. During his term as Dachuan's village
head, he was joined by a group of elderly Kongs in rebuilding the
Confucius temple. Once the temple was completed, he became
its chief manager.

The new Party secretary also played an important role in the
rebuilding of the Confucius temple. To make a temple site available, he reassigned land allotments affecting 30 households in
the village in order to create a site within the crowded residential
district. He gave up his position as the village's Party secretary
in 1993, when he became a salesman marketing Yellow River
carp raised in the local fish ponds. Already a fish-hatching specialist, he was said to be the fifth-richest person in Dachuan.
In 1993, he joined a five-member committee appointed by the
managers of the Confucius temple to expand the enrollment of
the local preschool, whose three-room schoolhouse was located
in the temple's courtyard.

Reform Through Hard Labor

Why were the new village cadres so interested in the Confucius temple? Some clues have already been suggested, but there
were other close connections between the new cadres and older
temple managers dating back to previous political movements.

The elderly temple managers had reached maturity at the onset of the Communist revolution. Nine of them completed their
educations at the primary school in Dachuan's old Confucius

temple. One went on to Lanzhou to attend a prestigious second-ary school, and two went on to a teachers' college, also in Lan-zhou. Not only had these educated men witnessed temple ritu-als before the Communist victory, but they had been in training to become "ritual performers" (li sheng) as part of their studies and, for three of them, as teachers at the temple's primary school. They were taught the principles and procedures of temple rituals by an older generation of educated villagers in the hope that they would carry on the tradition of offering sacrifices to Confucius. Four of these men were assistants at a 1949 temple ceremony attended by representatives of the entire Kong lineage. That was the last lineage-wide ceremony dedicated to the worship of Con-fucius until 1984.

With a lapse of 35 years, the managers of the new Confucius temple were the last Kongs to have received a classical educa-tion. Like other elites of the Kong lineage, most of them had been politically stigmatized. One related in interviews that during land reform he was classified as a poor peasant, a desirable class background. But in 1954, because he had once belonged to a Kuo-mintang youth organization, he was relabeled a "historical counterrevolutionary." He was fired from his position at a pri-mary school and had to return to Dachuan, where in the early 1960's he was put in charge of a special labor unit made up of people in four undesirable categories: landlords, rich peasants, counterrevolutionaries, and "evildoers" or "bad elements" (huai fen zi). The last category covered a mixed bag of characters rang-ing from religious practitioners to people who stole things from the collectives. Known as "the four kinds of bad elements" (si lei fen zi), these people were required, usually along with their wives and sometimes even their children, to work in a "labor-reform squad," whose tasks villagers from favorable class back-grounds would decline unless well compensated. These tasks included street-cleaning, transporting manure from pig sties, setting out stone stools for film showings, running errands for village cadres, and carrying heavy water containers to irri-gate distant fields. The agricultural chores were generally low-paying; the others were considered a compulsory part of thought reform.

"It was the 'four bad elements' who cultivated Dachuan's fruits of socialism," one former member of this special labor unit told me with an edge of sarcasm. Older villagers estimated that more than 200 people had worked, for different durations, in the village's "labor-reform squad." Its most consistent members were from fourteen households that had been classified during land reform as "landlords" or "rich peasants." Another sizable pool of free laborers consisted of people who had worked in the village administration or as low-ranking officials and army officers before the Communist takeover. There were also people who had been discovered saying or doing the wrong thing at the wrong time and were punished by assignment to the labor-reform team. The children of these people also suffered; their prospects for marriage, work points, and education were severely constricted by their parents' or grandparents' misfortunes.

New Village Cadres and Elderly Temple Managers

All three village cadres who took over the village's finances, administration, and Party organization after the downfall of the old Party secretary were from politically problematic or socially stigmatized families. One had suffered because of his father, who was discovered smoking opium during the Cultural Revolution. The father's secret addiction, exposed by neighbors and denounced at communal meetings, brought upon his son and daughter public shame and a reduction in their work points. Another cadre's father had also been humiliated at mass rallies, partly because he was accused of having close ties to other people from faulty family backgrounds and partly because he was the son of a key member of the local Big Sword society, a man who had been beheaded by the Communist government during a campaign against secret religious societies. The third village cadre had an uncle who was detained in 1969 on a charge of having bribed a government official during land reform to avoid being labeled a landlord. The bribery charge was prompted by a report filed by Dachuan's former Party secretary, and the detention led to a ten-year prison term. As a young man, he witnessed the arrest of his uncle, the confiscation of thirty rooms belonging to his uncle and father, and the rally staged in the village to denounce his uncle. After he assumed a key position in the village's cadre system, he himself was shrewd enough not to use his newfound power to press for the restoration of the family property seized during the Cultural Revolution. This property first fell under collective ownership and then was privatized during recollectivization. To reclaim it would have meant offending many people in Dachuan.[2]

I first got to know the new generation of village cadres during my 1989 research. In a sense I had to know them, for it was through them that I could conduct a study of the socioeconomic and ecological impact of the reservoir. It was also through them that I later became acquainted with the elderly managers of Dachuan's Confucius temple.

As mentioned in Chapter 3, fourteen men took a vow before taking charge of the temple-rebuilding project. With the completion of the temple, they became its managers. Only one of them, the chief of the vow-takers, was in his late thirties. The others were in their sixties and seventies. Of the thirteen elderly temple managers, ten had been disgraced for political reasons during the Maoist era.

In meetings with a former school teacher, at a straw shelter where he stayed day and night in summer to guard his family's orchard, he spoke of what it meant for a person with a college degree to have been classified as a "counterrevolutionary" and to have lost the teaching job he loved. Although another temple manager, a genealogist living in the nearby village of Huangci, met with me only once, he spent the whole night talking about what Dachuan looked like before resettlement, how his family was evicted when the reservoir was built, and the circumstances in which his father's collection of poems, paintings, temple couplets, and local genealogies was burned during the Cultural Revolution.

The deputy chief of the vow-takers spent many hours discussing the failings of the collective farming system. He had been a district head in charge of several people's communes, the official mentioned earlier who was dismissed from office in 1961 when it was found that some 300 people had starved to death in his district. A work team made up of officials from Beijing and Lanzhou forced him to make a self-criticism on stage, in front of about 3,000 people, many of whom had lost family members to starvation in the Great Leap famine. In describing this rally, he said:

> The people in the audience were angry. They thought I had a lot to eat while they did not. They were grinding their teeth with hate. They demanded that I be beheaded. In the end, the masses gave me a chance to live. Many people in the crowd started sobbing when I told them that I could not save even my own family. My wife, one of our sons, my brother, his wife, and their son all died of starvation back in Dachuan. My brother's wife was shamed to death. She was hungry and stole a handful of vegetables from the public dining hall. The cook caught her eating those rotten vegetables. He kicked and cursed her right in front of other men and women, old and young. She came back home weeping and went to sleep. She never woke up again.

In their own ways, both the younger village cadres and the older managers of the Confucius temple related in interviews from 1989 to 1993 a story of humiliation but also of regained dignity. Their prior experience of humiliation and persecution helps clarify why they banded together to rebuild the Confucius temple, and why local politics and temple politics were deeply entangled to the point of being nearly inseparable. As survivors of the Communist revolution, they had climbed to prominent positions in their community from failed careers, dismembered families, and political stigmatization. For these people, there was no more effective form of vindication of their personal honor than forging an alliance to rebuild, protect, and manage a sacred landmark whose fate in the recent past was so symbolically identical to their own.

6

Memory of Ritual Language

From Ritual to Memory, and Back

Growing up in a culture entails learning how to handle one's body and language to replicate appropriate modes of ritual behavior. An outcome of this learning process is the development of "habitual memory," a term coined by Paul Connerton in reference to the conditioned mind that allows easy adjustment to the requirements of ritual whenever they arise (Connerton 1989: 72–104). With frequent practice, this habituation leads to a routinized recall of proper forms of ritual movement and speech. "In habitual memory," explains Connerton, "the past is, as it were, sedimented in the body" (Connerton 1989: 72). Put in less abstract terms, we know how to control our body and language in a ritually suitable manner because we have done it so often that it has become second nature, an embodied reaction. Although Connerton touches on the possibility of memory loss and its ritual consequences, he does not discuss what it might take to recover memory of ritual propriety should it fade or be lost altogether. Under normal circumstances, we could assume, salvaging that memory means relearning rituals within the structures of religious life. But if these structures have been shattered by political persecution, as was the case in Maoist

China, the relearning process becomes considerably more problematic. This was the situation of the Kongs, once restraints on religion were relaxed in the post-Mao period.

As recounted in the last chapter, Dachuan's former Party secretary was responsible for the conversion of a carpenters' workshop into a provisional ancestor shrine in 1984. By most accounts, the first and second ceremonies performed there were not unlike the shrine itself—simple, makeshift, and experimental. Before the Party secretary could improve on this, he was pressured to resign his official post in 1986. Subsequently, he lost control of the provisional ancestor shrine to the new village head, who then joined with thirteen elderly Kongs to rebuild Dachuan's Confucius temple. Before the temple could be built, the provisional shrine had to serve as the site for a revived temple-based ceremony that had not been performed for more than three decades. The former lineage elders who had been directly responsible for the performance of the ceremony had died by the mid-1980's. Fortunately, a number of elderly men still living in Dachuan and other Kong villages had been ritual assistants in their youth. The new village head wisely decided to consult these men.

The reconstruction of the temple ceremony, first at the provisional shrine and then at the rebuilt Confucius temple, was a gradual process. Its completion was marked in 1991, when the temple managers produced a ritual handbook, written by hand on 52 pages and divided into eighteen texts, setting down the results of their work of the previous six years.[1] The handbook offers moral, historical, and technical exegetics for the ritual ceremony. It is a remarkable work, noteworthy for its many historical references, formal literary style, arcane language, and complicated names for ritual objects.

This chapter examines the ritual handbook as a guide to the methods employed by the temple managers to deal with the linguistic dimensions of ritual. We begin with a description of the ritual handbook's genesis and then shift to an analysis of three aspects of the Kongs' ritual language, namely, its literary style, its writing system, and its methods of vocalization.

Memory Rehearsal and Ritual Reconstruction

The ritual handbook was produced through a series of meetings that I prefer to describe as "memory rehearsals." To begin, the vow-takers in Dachuan were uncertain about the basic structure of the ceremony. In the hope that genealogies might contain useful information or even comprehensive ritual guidelines, three of the temple managers searched for genealogical records. They found numerous ritual references in two large genealogies, one of which was written in 1905. However, they could not find a ready set of ceremonial terms and instructions. With the time for the annual ceremony approaching, the temple managers called a special meeting in Dachuan, which was attended by more than 30 elderly men from other Kong villages. For three days, they discussed what each of them remembered of the ceremony. Most of these men had been entrusted with specific ritual duties. Among them, for instance, was a former butcher of sacrificial animals and a former ceremonial flute player. Another had been responsible for carrying incense sticks and yellow paper to the lineage elders when prompted by the chief liturgist of the ceremony and by the leading liturgists in charge of the ceremony's individual rites. But since nobody had an overview of the ceremony, the participants in this meeting were compelled to concentrate on recalling their own duties, demonstrating how individual ritual acts had been performed and what words had been uttered by the leading liturgists.

One product of this rehearsal-like meeting was a written outline of the ceremony's five sacrificial rites. In the first, called "Greeting the Sacrifices" (*ying sheng li*), food and drink were transported to the temple. The sacrifices were prepared in the kitchen of a residential compound and then carried to the temple grounds in a procession through the community's main streets.

The second rite, called "Greeting the Arrival of the Holy Spirits" (*ying sheng jia li*), consisted of chanting a written prayer calling on the spirits of the ancestors to descend to the temple and enjoy the sacrificial food. The next three were a sequence labeled the "offering rites" (*xian li*) and took place inside the temple's main hall. These offering rites included the pouring of liquor onto the ground, the presentation of cooked meat, the chanting of memorial elegies, the burning of incense and joss papers, and the demonstration of gratitude by bows and kowtows.

In my interviews with ten of the fourteen temple managers in 1992, each one was asked separately whether the ceremony before 1949 had really consisted of five rites or whether this was a recent innovation. The implicit suggestion that the ceremony they were performing might in any way deviate from past rites was met with uniform denials. Their replies had a decidedly rehearsed tone. The ceremony, they said, had always had five sacrificial rites. This is what they remembered and they had reconstructed it accordingly.

Another problem the temple managers faced was uncertainty over the ritual names for the sacrificial animals. They knew that a pig, sheep, chicken, and rabbit were required. But they did not know the exact ritual names for these animals. In the 1905 genealogy, they found a list of 32 names for ritual offerings ranging from bread and drink to sacrificial meat. On closer examination, however, this list was of limited usefulness because it was intended to show the proper arrangement of offerings on the sacrificial altar, not the proper terms for ritual speech. This means that the sacrificial animals it listed were identified by their ordinary names. For example, one sacrificial animal was listed simply as *zhu rou*, or "pig flesh." This is an everyday word for pork, unsuitable for ritual utterance. Eventually, the oldest person in Dachuan—he was 83 when I interviewed him in 1992—came up with the proper sacrificial names: *gang lie*, the "hot-tempered one," for the pig; *rou mao*, the "soft-haired one," for the sheep; *han yin*, the "clear-voiced one," for the chicken; and *ming shi*, the "sharp-eyed one," for the rabbit. The man who recalled this set of ritual terms had been an assistant liturgist at the old Confucius temple whose duty it was to carry small portions of the sacrificial meat with chopsticks from the top of the central altar to a wooden plate below it. He had to be able to select the appropriate meat, he stressed, when its ritual name was called out by the chief liturgist directing the rite.

A third problem was what memorial elegies should be read in the temple ceremony. These elegies, in which the living extol the heroic deeds and upright characters of the dead, are a means of assuring the enshrined spirits that they are not forgotten. By reading the memorial elegies and then burning them, the living call on the dead to accept the sacrificial offerings. Through these acts of communion, the living provide the dead with nourishment to sustain them in the other world, while the dead protect the welfare of the living in this world. In contrast to their decisiveness regarding the names of the sacrificial animals, the temple managers allowed the memorial elegies to be revised and improved every year. The final versions of the elegies were a work of historical imagination and literary innovation, and yet hardly arbitrary.

In revising the elegies, the temple managers benefited a great deal from their childhood education. Nine of them had gone beyond the primary school level of "classical education" in the pre-Communist period, which means that a key part of their basic schooling had consisted of memorizing ancient poems, classical texts, and Confucian quotations. Memorization skills were honed through recitation drills and long hours of lessons in calligraphy. In other words, they had been rigorously trained to commit texts to memory and to retrieve them in a well-written form. By pooling their knowledge of history, genealogies, and classical education, the temple managers continued to refine the elegies during the preparations for each annual ceremony. Gradually, the content of the elegies was enriched as new information was brought into the process. In 1986, the elegy dedicated to the founding ancestors of the Kong lineage in Gansu contained only a few dozen words; by 1991 it had expanded to 370 characters.

In the late spring of 1991, Dachuan's new Confucius temple entered its final phase of construction with the installation of its central cross-beam. The work on the essential elements of the ritual ceremony entered a crucial phase. In the next four months, the temple managers held another round of intensive rehearsal-like meetings to standardize the ritual texts and procedures they had worked out. The result was the 52-page ritual handbook that, in September 1991, guided the first ceremony of ancestor worship at the new temple.

Language, Writing, and Performance

Ritual ceremonies are rarely silent performances. The language of ritual varies from culture to culture, and yet often involves the utterance of a distinctive set of memorized or written words. As early as 1909, Arnold van Gennep wrote in his famous book *The Rites of Passage* that a special language was employed in most of the religious ceremonies he examined. In some cases, the language included an entire vocabulary unknown or unusual in the larger society. In others, it reflected a prohibition against using certain words in everyday language. "This phenomenon should be considered of the same order as the change of dress, mutilations and special foods, i.e., as a perfectly normal differentiating procedure" (van Gennep [1909] 1960: 169).

In more recent anthropological writings, ritual language is recognized as a sacred domain of myths, a contribution to the exalted image of liturgists, and an arcane means of communication with saviors, deities, prophets, or ancestors (see Firth 1967; Fortune 1963; George 1990: 2–23; Malinowski 1935; Tambiah 1985: 17–59). Above all, ritual words are considered an inseparable component of ritual actions. As Edmund Leach has aptly put it, "It is not the case that words are one thing and the rite another. The utterance of the words itself is a ritual" (1966: 407).

The observations cited above apply to the Kong ritual language. A close look at the Kong ritual handbook reveals that its written language is rigid, extremely formalized, and very repetitive. Its sentence structure, choice of words, and parallel epigrams, for example, give the impression of an archaic form of speech. Its literary attributes and cultural implications are difficult to appreciate once translated from Chinese. Still, the effort is worthwhile for analytical purposes. The following translation is of the beginning of a text called *ji wen*, a memorial elegy chanted during the ceremony that calls on the spirit of Confucius to accept the ritual offerings:

> Oh, Confucius, a great man! Oh, Confucius, the greatest of all men. Before Confucius, there were no men like Confucius. After Confucius, there were few men like Confucius. The noble men before Confucius's birth were not as noble as Confucius. The honorable men after Confucius's death were not as honorable as Confucius. Morality, wisdom, and insight all derive from Confucius. China and the world have only one Confucius. In 10,000 years, the paramount teacher of mankind is found in Confucius. All the five continents of the world aspire to the Harmonious Community preached by Confucius. All the virtues of the world are personified by Confucius.

Like the other texts in the handbook, this elegy is written in *wen yan*, which Western scholars usually refer to as "classical Chinese" or "learned language," in contrast to "modern Chinese" or "everyday language." Although it is not uncommon for texts written in *wen yan* to be recited or quoted orally, this classical language is seldom, if ever, used by anyone in conversation or for practical purposes in daily life.

Somewhat like Latin in the West, *wen yan* is more of an academic or religious accomplishment than a natural form of expression. In imperial China, it was strictly confined to the scholarly world for transcribing official, literary, and historical documents. Working with it required a profound knowledge of lexicography, metric rules, tonal similarities, and other devices. When an emperor's written instructions were announced to

commoners across the empire, local interpreters had to be found
to convert the decrees into the vernacular and regional dialects
(Mair 1985: 325–59). Long associated with the imagery of logographic characters, the scholarly art of calligraphy, civil service
examinations, and court documents (see Chao Yuen-ren 1968;
Teng & Fairbank 1963: 251–58; Rawski 1979), *wen yan* was elitist in nature, and as such came under attack with the fall of the
Manchu empire and the advent of the Republic in 1912. Along
with Confucian values and institutions, it was regarded as an
obstacle to China's entering the modern world and blamed for
the country's underdevelopment in science and technology. In
a literary revolution during and after World War I, Chinese intellectuals pushed for the replacement of *wen yan* with *bai hua*,
"vernacular language." They advocated that everyday forms of
speech become the written medium for all communications, including scholarship. "Many joined in this revolutionary movement, which denied the superior value of the old literary style.
The use of *bai hua* spread rapidly; the tyranny of the classics
had been broken" (Fairbank 1992: 266). It should be immediately
pointed out, however, that the use of "vernacular language" did
not apply to the transcription of religious texts, which, as demonstrated by the Kong ritual handbook, has continued to rely on
"classical" Chinese.

Reinforcing the Kongs' use of *wen yan* was the traditional
writing system they chose for transcribing the ritual handbook
and the memorial elegies to be read and burned during the ceremony. This writing system has been discouraged by the Chinese
government since the 1960's, when a nationwide program was
undertaken to promote simplified characters called *jian ti zi*.
The new script was intended to replace the traditional form of
writing, known as *fan ti zi*, "complex characters." The basic
technique for simplification is to reduce the number of strokes
written to form a character (see Cheng 1977: 314–54; DeFrancis
1977; Sampson 1985: 145–71). One consequence of the writing
reform is that those young enough to have learned the new system at school are bound to have great difficulty reading texts

written in the old script. Writing the old script is even more difficult. Classical novels and important texts printed before the language reform have had to be reprinted in the simplified script. Another problem is that overseas Chinese and the people of Taiwan and Hong Kong have not accepted the new writing system.[2] Older people in mainland China who were educated in the traditional system can shift between the old and new scripts with enviable ease. Two such persons are Kong Xiangguo in Dachuan and Kong Fanjun in the village of Zhongzhuang, who edited and copied the texts in the Kong ritual handbook.

In the annual ceremony for the worship of Confucius and the local founding ancestors, the reading of memorial elegies was based on stylized speech. For one thing, the elegies were chanted in an unnatural falsetto. The rise and fall of chanted words was punctuated by rhythmic pulses and protracted syllables. Most people attending the ceremony could not understand the chanted elegies because of the artificially high pitch, the tonal changes, and the rhythmic alterations, not to mention that the meaning of the chanted elegies was already obscure because they were written in *wen yan*. Despite this, the leading liturgists pressed on and nobody seemed to mind.

The Meaning of an Inscrutable Ritual Speech

Normally, we speak in order to communicate and the utterance of sounds is meant to convey clear messages. But this is not the case in the Kongs' chanting of the ritual elegies. Whether in its written or spoken form, the Kong ritual language is not clearly intelligible to any ordinary person unless he has been educated in classical Chinese or trained to play a direct part in the ceremony. But this is not to say that the incomprehensibility of the ritual words robs the ceremonial performance of ideological significance. The participants perceive the ritual language at a different level, which must be analyzed within the wider context of village life, especially religious practice.

In an interview, Kong Fanjun and Kong Xiangguo, who had

copied the ritual book by hand, insisted that the simplified script would have been inappropriate and that they followed "a correct way of composing ritual texts." Pressed for an explanation, they looked at me as if I were from another planet. Ritual texts had always been written in the old script, one of them answered in a slightly irritated tone.

Having failed to glean a satisfying explanation from Kong Xiangguo and Kong Fanjun, I began paying closer attention to writings in the village and noticed that the words on secular objects, such as account books, drug prescriptions, and public notices of various kinds, were all written in the simplified script, and in the vernacular language. By contrast, the traditional script was consistently used for religious objects, including ancestral tablets in household shrines, divination stalks, genealogical booklets, room-sized charts of ancestral names, poetic couplets for weddings and the lunar New Year, prayers for the birth of sons or the recovery of health, talismans attached to the highest beam of a house, and paper money and coffin decorations for death rituals. Furthermore, the writing on religious objects was all in the classical language.

This division of secular and religious writings means that the Kongs' choice of language for their ritual handbook and for conducting the temple ceremony is not an isolated case. It has its roots in the village's broader patterns of religious life, in which an older writing system and traditional modes of literary expressions are preferred. Once the Kong ritual language is seen within this context, its amalgam of a complex literary style, traditional script, and stylized speech can be explained by the public perception it creates—as an archaic, refined, and sacred language. The use of classical Chinese exemplifies cultivated learning on the part of the temple managers, the traditional script is customary for religious objects, and the stylized speech safeguards the sacredness of ritual performance by rejecting everyday language. Each device contributes to the ideal of maintaining purity in a ceremony intended to achieve communion with spiritual beings. Before the ceremony can begin, all objects and persons involved must be purified. This involves the ritual washing of hands, the donning of new or at least freshly cleaned clothes, the polishing of incense burners, and a procession to transport sacrifices from a residential compound to a sacred altar in the temple.

And language, too, must be purified. To use secular language in a religious ceremony would be akin to entering the holy place with unwashed hands or disheveled dress. It must be avoided lest it defile the rites. Similar reasoning has promoted the use of Hebrew by Jews, Latin in the Roman Catholic Church into the 1960's, Vedic Sanskrit by Hindus, Pali by Buddhists in Southeast Asia, and classical Arabic by Muslims in different parts of the world. Each case involved an archaic and sacred language, dis- tanced from the secular world. And, more important, the lan- guage symbolizes orthodoxy and authority because it implicitly suggests that the rites and ritual words have been transmitted faithfully from the past to the present (Tambiah 1985: 17–59).

A key aspect of the Kong ritual language lies in its contribu- tion to a body of esoteric knowledge. Access to it requires not only special training but institutional approval. The leading lit- urgists of the Kong ceremony were either the temple managers or elders they had selected to read the memorial elegies and to deliver ceremonial instructions. This means that the middle- aged men who served as assistants to the leading liturgists were at a double disadvantage: They were denied access to the ritual handbook and given only piecemeal information about the rites, and they needed time to become familiar with the ceremonial procedures. As part of the price they had to pay for having been given an honorable role in a local event of great importance, they had to stand back, observe their elders, and commit to memory as best they could all that was being said and done.[3]

The Kong Ritual Language and Its Broader Implications

In this chapter, we have seen how individual memories were shared and ritual dilemmas resolved in the rehearsal-like meetings of temple managers and elderly men with some ceremonial experience. We have also discussed the role of genealogical texts and oral memory in determining correct names for sacrificial offerings. Rote knowledge derived from the old "classical education" contributed to the composing of memorial elegies. Whether in the employment of the three elements of Kong ritual language or in the resolution of the three ritual dilemmas, there was a constant interplay of orally communicated, textually based, and bodily sedimented memories.

The influence of written texts on the Kongs' recall of ritual language was evidently strong. Yet, we should not exaggerate it. The memorization of classical texts and the repeated copying of those texts by the temple managers in their childhood years served to impress the written characters on mind and body. The written materials were mastered through constant recitation and calligraphy exercises. After more than three decades of radical socialism, most of the original texts the Kongs once used were gone, but at least fragments survived in the minds of those who once memorized them. By the sharing of individual memories in their meetings and with the help of some existing texts, shards of ritual knowledge were pieced together. This knowledge was then formalized in writing with the appearance of the ritual handbook. But even this carefully written document cannot provide guidance on the chanting of memorial elegies, the core of the ritual ceremony. The ability to deliver the intonations, the artificially high pitch, and the rhythmic pauses can only be achieved through rehearsals and live performances. That is to say, these skills are preserved in the realm of oral and embodied memories.

In connection with the Kong ritual language, the research by Walter Ong and Jack Goody should be mentioned (Goody & Watt 1968; Goody 1977, 1986, 1987; Ong 1977, [1982] 1988). Their writings on the mnemonic implications of orality and literacy are thought-provoking—as in, for example, their discussions of writing as "an instrument of secrecy and power" (Goody 1986: 236; Ong [1982] 1988: 93). However, some generalizations made by Ong and Goody on the mnemonic impacts of orality and literacy also contain debatable assertions, one of which is their assessment of the Chinese writing system. Particularly relevant to the Kong case is Ong's observation that "the step to alphabetization [of the Chinese script] will be short and, in this writer's considered opinion, inevitable and rapid, however sad and disastrous." The precondition for the death of the Chinese script, he says, will be met "when all the speakers of Chinese learn Mandarin Chinese, which is now being taught, more or less satisfactorily, as obligatory to everyone in the People's Republic of China, and being taught in Taiwan as well" (Ong 1977: 33–44; [1982] 1988: 86–87).

In making this prediction, Ong draws on Goody to explain his belief in the inevitable shift from writing in pictographic characters to the widespread use of an alphabetic system in China. "The K'anghsi dictionary of Chinese in A.D. 1761 lists 40,545 characters," Ong quotes a passage from an earlier work by Goody. "Few Chinese or Sinologists know them all, or ever did. . . . Such a script is basically time-consuming and elitist. There can be no doubt that the characters will be replaced by the Roman alphabet as soon as all the people in the People's Republic of China master the same language" (Ong [1982] 1988: 87; also see Goody and Watt 1968: 113).

There are two issues Ong and Goody have obviously failed to consider. First, if the criterion for literacy in Chinese is that one is familiar with more than 40,000 characters, then no Chinese has ever been literate; but this is absurd. Second, the promotion of so-called Mandarin or "standard" Chinese has shown no sign yet of replacing regional languages, partly because the local languages are intimately bound up with regional customs and identity.

Given that the writing system Ong and Goody cite by way of a dictionary published in 1761 is the traditional script, one should add that the Communists' demotion of this script has not expelled it from religious life. The use of the traditional script is found in all kinds of religious writings in contemporary mainland China. What this means is that the Chinese government's writing reform has, ironically, endowed the older script with a religious quality it did not enjoy in the past. To borrow a phrase from Sally Moore and Barbara Meyerhoff, the older script has become essentially "a traditionalizing instrument" (1977; quoted by Tambiah 1985: 132). Coupled with the use of classic Chinese and stylized speech, it functions as a legitimating tool and a cultural device to encourage the belief in the authenticity of religious rituals and texts. While the older script was used for secular purposes in what is by Chinese standards a very recent past, it has become, thanks to official intervention in the People's Republic, a vehicle for sacred knowledge.[4] At the village level, those who can still use the older script along with classical Chinese to compose religious texts are thus able to acquire a recycled instrument of authority.

7

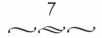

Memory of Genealogical Retainers

A Troublesome Source of Data

Those who have consulted Chinese genealogies in demographic research know all too well what exasperating documents they can be. Describing his study of genealogies discovered in Taiwan, Stevan Harrell declares: "With the exception of certain local and specialized populations, there exist very few population registers suitable for Cambridge-style family reconstruction. If we are to study population process in a wide variety of localities over a considerable time span, we seem to have only one kind of source in any abundance: the lineage or clan genealogy" (Harrell 1987: 53). However, Harrell warns us, the Chinese genealogy is an extremely frustrating source of demographic data. One problem is the omission of the names of anyone who died young, never married, or became a monk. A similar observation is offered by Johanna Meskill (1970: 139–62), who writes that it is extremely difficult, if not impossible, to estimate mortality rates on the basis of genealogies because of their exclusion of uxorilocally married-in husbands and children adopted from families with other surnames.

Scholars seeking information besides demographic data in Chinese genealogies encounter other maddening problems. A record keeper may have gone so far as to use the full name of each man of a descent group, and may even have separated charts of names from one another to indicate which people belonged to the same segmentary units of a lineage. Still, few scholars, especially anthropologists, are ready to assume that kinship labels represent the reality of interpersonal relationships.[1] Occasionally, certain kinds of documents can be very suggestive, such as texts on the management of corporate estates. But in the final analysis, it is as if the researchers were forced to watch a play through a closed curtain with enough holes to allow the conviction that a play is being performed, but with no hole large enough to allow the stage and actors to be seen in their entirety. Thousands of Chinese genealogies are thus stored in libraries in China, Taiwan, Hong Kong, Japan, and the United States "to baffle scholars with their size, complexity and frequent defiance of meaningful analysis" (H. Baker 1979: 68).

What does the Chinese genealogy aim for, given that it is such a capricious source of empirical evidence for scholars? Obviously not designed for the convenience of scientific scrutiny, it focuses only on matters important to the common descent group. Instituted in the third century A.D., regular compilation of genealogies was at first confined to the ruling class—royal families and high-ranking officials (Liu Liming 1993: 135–57). This monopoly persisted until the Song dynasty (960–1279), and it was only around the eleventh century that private genealogies began to be produced by local descent groups (Hu 1948: 45). The standards for these genealogies were laid down and promulgated by scholars, notably Ouyang Xiu (1007–72) and Su Xun (1009–66). These men of letters were among a group of scholars who have been commonly described by contemporary historians as Neo-Confucianists.

What the Neo-Confucianists stressed was the weight of the primary groups, the importance of family discipline, and the centrality of self-restraint, which in their eyes were three basic and indispensable means of achieving social stability (Ebrey 1986: 35; Liu Hui-chen 1959: 65; see also de Bary 1959: 25–49;

Metzger 1977, Bol 1992). Genealogical compilation was considered by these Neo-Confucianists as an effective means of
achieving family cohesion and thus social stability. However,
only a small number of genealogies were produced in the Song
period. Mostly written for prominent lineages, they were limited to *shi xi tu*, "charts of descent."

The real flowering of genealogy writing in Chinese society at
large did not come until the latter part of the Ming dynasty
(1371–1644), when it became standard practice to incorporate in
genealogies precepts of moral conduct, lineage history, marriage
regulations, inheritance rules, ritual instructions, and so forth.
One factor that may have contributed to this development was
the widening acceptance of Neo-Confucian ideology during the
Ming period. The practice of writing genealogies continued into
the Manchu period (1644–1911) without fundamental change.
As private records, these genealogical documents were shielded
from public view until the 1930's, when amidst great political
upheavals and constant warfare, thousands of them became
available to book dealers (Hu 1948: 51; Meskill 1970: 40) and
subsequently made their way into Chinese, Japanese and American libraries.[2]

Genealogical Writing and Practical Kinship

Patricia Ebrey, who has studied the rise of Neo-Confucianism
during the Song period, argues that the appearance of genealogies
among common descent groups can be traced to the political
strategy adopted by educated elites "in an effort to reform kinship practices among members of their social class (*shi da fu*)"
(Ebrey 1986: 35). She names a number of Song intellectuals who
either set out to produce genealogies themselves or wrote com-
mentaries on the moral and technical aspects of genealogical
compilation. These writings "provided the ideological justifi-
cation for promoting descent group organization for the next
several centuries" (Ebrey 1986: 35).

Along the same line, Robert Hymes says that genealogy writing made political sense, even for those who had never previously belonged to any corporate kinship groups. "It [genealogical compilation] may often have been accompanied by immediate efforts to establish the entire unit as a practical group" (Hymes 1986: 122). To clarify Hymes's statement, the production of genealogies had the potential to create agnatic kinship groups that might have never or only loosely existed. The publicly proclaimed origin of descent did not always create actual ties of kinship, but was available for forging networks should the practical need for kinship arise.

Also proceeding from a historical perspective, Eberhard and Meskill have emphasized Chinese genealogies as "retrospective constructions." That is to say, many lineage and clan genealogies have been revised to underscore connections with more powerful brethren in order to enhance unity or prestige and to seek protection from the bureaucratic system (Eberhard 1966: 206–8; Meskill 1970: 110). Certainly, not all descent groups compiled genealogies. Probably only a small number did. But this small number may well have been a substantial minority, especially in the lower Yangzi River region where, until the Communist takeover of China, active commerce and a high concentration of educated people bolstered the genealogical enterprise.

Descent groups with extensive genealogies nearly always included among their constituents a relatively large number of scholar-officials, whose textual knowledge and historical imagination enabled them to seek out illustrious ancestors. It is in this regard that Hsiao Kung-chuan described the compilation of genealogical records as "a gentry institution" (Hsiao 1960: 333). By contrast, descent groups of more modest circumstances often lacked deep genealogies with information about many descending generations.

With regard to the overall social implications of Chinese genealogies, the most elucidating observation comes from Maurice Freedman, who promoted, as early as 1966, the study of genealogical data from a sociological point of view. The few people examining such data, Freedman said, tended to see them primarily as sources of demographic, institutional, and biographical information. "A genealogy is much more than that," he said. "It is a set of claims to origin and relationships, a charter, a map of dispersion, a framework for wide-ranging social organization, a blueprint for action. It is a political statement—and therefore a perfect subject for the anthropologists" (1966: 31).

Freedman's characterization of the genealogy as a political statement was recently reiterated by James Watson, who concedes that anthropologists may have underestimated the compilation of genealogies as a means of uniting people. He interprets genealogy writing as a "structure of mental attitudes" reflecting political strategies (Watson 1986: 287). To rephrase his point, the genealogical enterprise is a polished form of manipulation of the past for a variety of social, economic, and political purposes.

Drawing on previous scholarship, I examine the use of genealogies by the Kongs from the perspective of social memory. This examination focuses on two events: The first is the reaction in Dachuan to the compilation of the Kong clan genealogy in Qufu in the 1930's; the second is the connection between genealogical records and the ritual handbook produced by the Dachuan temple managers in 1991. A principal assumption underpinning this discussion is that genealogies are a vehicle for forging political alliances and making sense of history. Indeed, I would claim that these goals are inseparable from genealogical compilation.

From Small Names to Big Names

Before setting out for my 1992 fieldwork, I went to Harvard University's Yenching Library to photocopy a section of the 1937 edition of the Kong clan genealogy (Kong Decheng 1937). It is essentially a name list of the Kongs in Yongjing, filled with entries for generational ranks, residential divisions, and places of settlement in Guangdong and Gansu from the eleventh century to the 1930's. This genealogical register helped me to design field interviews, and my informants were amazed that I could name people who had been dead for decades or longer. At first they assumed that these names had come up in other interviews. However, it did not take them long to discover the real source of my information. The village's chief accountant, an intelligent man in his late twenties, noticed that I had been reading my photocopied genealogical register at his home, where I ate, slept, typed field notes, and conducted some of my interviews. The register did not arouse his interest until people began mentioning to him my disconcerting ability to cite names of long-departed villagers. One night, the accountant asked his mother to prepare three dishes for us—a boiled chicken, a full plate of carp, and pork with shredded potatoes—a feast in this village. He brought out a bottle of throat-scorching liquor and pulled off the metal cap with his teeth. After the gasolinelike spirits were poured into a small kettle, we were in for a finger game that required the loser of two consecutive games to down a full shot-glass. When two-thirds of the spirits had been consumed, my host launched into an animated monologue about friendship and how well I was liked by the local villagers. He concluded the compliments with a special request: Would I be kind enough to give the genealogical register to the Confucius temple?

I never learned whether the accountant had been instructed by the temple managers to get hold of the genealogical register, and if so why they did not ask me directly for it. In any case, I had intended to leave the register in Dachuan, where it truly belonged. After my host brought it to the temple the next afternoon, a group of middle-aged and elderly men assembled. Kong Xiangguo, the temple watchman, was reading and explaining to the crowd the names recorded in the register. Explanations were necessary because all the names were *da ming*, or "big names," with which some of the people in the crowd were unfamiliar. These formal, prescribed "big names" denote generational ranks. In Dachuan, they are often bestowed when a person is enrolled in school or about to be married. But many villagers have only *xiao ming*, or "small names," which are informal, given at birth, and carried through childhood into adolescence, occasionally even into old age.

The rendering of "big names" once followed strict rules set down by the Kong clan council in Qufu. Accordingly, a "big name" comprises three characters: the surname, a generational marker, and a personal name, in that order. An example is the name of Kong Decheng, the former Yansheng Duke who now lives in Taiwan. Kong is of course his surname. De, the Chinese word for "virtue," denotes the seventy-seventh generation of the Kongs, to which he was born. Cheng, which means "accomplishment," is his personal name, chosen by his parents. From 1398 to 1912, the council depended on emperors to provide the characters to mark the Kong generations. Every male of the clan was in theory named from this officially sanctioned list of characters; boys named otherwise would be omitted from the clan genealogy. When this list of generational names began to be exhausted in 1920, the clan council added another twenty characters.

The people who gathered at Dachuan's Confucius temple to see the genealogical register I had brought from Harvard already knew the prescribed list of generational names, although not all knew how it originated. In 1992, roughly one-third of the male adults in Dachuan had "big names" that complied with the prescribed list. The others had only "small names" or individually invented names. This indicates that the rules for distinguishing generations by name were not strictly observed.

Charters of Descent and Political Alliance

The genealogical document read by the temple watchman was compiled in 1930 and printed in 1937, on the basis of a local register prepared by the Kongs in the Dachuan area in response to an appeal by the clan council in Qufu to provide local records for the making of the clan genealogy. Each local register was required to adhere to the fixed order of generational names set by the clan council. Four well-educated members of the Kong lineage in the Dachuan area were charged with assigning big names to those who had been using small names.

Dachuan's response to Qufu's plan to update the clan genealogy supports the argument of scholars such as Patricia Ebrey and James Watson that in Chinese society, genealogies could be a powerful tool for uniting people. In answer to Qufu's call for local genealogies, the educated and probably rich as well as powerful Kongs in the Dachuan area embarked on a project that must have been highly significant to ordinary members of the lineage as well. The assigning of formalized names to those people bearing only small names marked a historical moment in which connections were forged between the educated elites and the less prominent members of the local lineage. Those who had been known only by their childhood names or nicknames were generally poor and uneducated.

The compilation of the local register offered Kongs of different socioeconomic positions an opportunity to celebrate their common identity. Even though the formalized names did not have the power to alter the local hierarchical structure, it must have been a memorable experience for a poor, illiterate man to be identified and included in the making of the clan genealogy. It may even have provided an illusion of equality. No matter how ephemeral, that illusion was a leveling device, a strategy to commemorate unity. Most important, Dachuan's response to Qufu's call for local registers established a tangible connection with the Kong clan council.

The communications between Qufu and Dachuan passed through Kong Qinghui, the merchant in Lanzhou who traveled twice to Qufu to obtain the clan genealogy. According to his memoir of the two trips to Qufu (Kong Qinghui 1948), he had received a notice from the clan council about the genealogy project in 1930. Once the local register was finished, he hired scholars in Lanzhou to revise it to accord with the style stipulated by the clan council. He then sent the revised register to Qufu and received a letter from the clan council confirming the descent claims in the local register. In 1935 the clan council, he said, asked the Kongs in Gansu to send a representative to Qufu for a conference on the genealogy project. This gathering was attended by representatives from throughout the country. In his memoir, Kong Qinghui expresses regret that business affairs kept him from attending the meeting. This suggests that he might have received an invitation letter from Qufu. Two days later, Kong Qinghui traveled to Qufu but failed to obtain a copy of the clan genealogy. In 1948, he made a second trip to Qufu and finally was given a copy. The arrival of the clan genealogy in Lanzhou was greeted by 22 leading members of the local Kong lineage. During their stay in Lanzhou, they threw a banquet in Kong Qinghui's honor, and a group photograph taken after the banquet was later included in his published memoir.

From Commemoration of Death to Celebration of Birth

Dachuan's contact with Qufu through genealogical compilation introduced a ritual ceremony that has direct relevance to this study—the celebration of Confucius's birthday. Before they joined the project organized by Qufu to compile what would become the largest extant genealogy in China, the ancestral ceremonies of the Kongs in Dachuan were held on these three occasions:

1. The lunar New Year holiday (*guonian*) was the time for individuals to offer food and drink at the tombs of their immediate ancestors. This graveside activity involved the close agnates who traced their lines of descent to a common ancestor five generations back.

2. The Spring Equinox (*chunfen*) was for the lineage's four segments to perform separate tomb rites to commemorate their early ancestors, concentrating on the four ancestors who came to Dachuan as brothers and founded the local lineage.

3. The Clear and Bright festival, Qingming, called for two types of ritual activities. The day before the festival, the lineage sent a group of people to a village named Yanjiawan to sweep the tomb of Kong Gongyou, the father of the four brothers who settled in Dachuan and became the founders of the local Kong lineage. The festival day itself was for a lineage-based ritual ceremony to be performed at Dachuan's Confucius temple, which

enshrined the spirit tablets of Confucius and six early local ancestors, five of whom I have mentioned—Kong Gongyou and his
four sons. The sixth was Kong Jiaxing, who came from Guangdong to Gansu and was the focal ancestor of the highest order.
His tomb, in the southern suburbs of Lanzhou, was cared for by
a group of Kongs who remained in or returned to the city. The
Kongs in the Dachuan area sacrificed not at his tomb, but to his
spirit tablet in the local Confucius temple.

In institutional terms, the ritual intensity progressed from
households to four lineage segments, leading up to a joint ceremony at the temple. The ritual sequence covered the early phase
of the year and was punctuated by three important dates. The
lunar New Year holiday is a time of great joy, but also a time to
show gratitude to the departed who brought the living into this
world. The Spring Equinox rite is related to the dualist *yin-yang*
theory, which associates life with daylight and death with night.
Hence the division of light and darkness into equal durations
during the Spring Equinox presents the shortest disparity between the dead and the living, making it a popular time to commemorate ancestors.[3] Qingming was derived from an official ritual dedicated to a courtier who allegedly starved himself to
death out of loyalty to his master (Xue 1991: 449–50). This festival gained popularity among commoners in the tenth century
(Chuang 1990: 149), and gradually became the occasion for a nationwide death ritual.

None of these ritual activities were meant to mark ancestors'
births.[4] And a careful reading of the genealogy produced by the
Kongs in 1905 indicates that as late as the turn of this century,
they had not yet developed any interest in celebrating the anniversary of Confucius's birth. This ten-volume genealogy has
three texts on the significance of ancestral rituals. However,
they all stress the importance of seasonal sacrifices, especially
during Qingming.

Ritual documents kept by the Kongs in Qufu also emphasize
seasonal sacrifices. In fact, seasonal sacrifices to Confucius were
ordained in official regulations (see, e.g., Feuchtwang 1977;

Kong Fanyin 1992). Since delegates from the imperial court during the Ming and Qing eras regularly visited the sage's hometown to offer sacrifices, they left behind numerous "memorial elegies" (ji wen), that is, ritual texts read aloud during the offering of sacrifices. Of the 30 of these elegies I have examined, the oldest dates back to 1331 and the most recent to 1909 (Kong Fanyin 1992: 80–85; Kong Zhaozeng 1934: 1, 19–27). Not a single elegy was delivered to mark the sage's birthday. The sacrifices presented were seasonal offerings. Above one-third of these sacrificial elegies were recited in the springtime, indicating that the vernal sacrifices were dominant over other seasonal offerings.

All of this suggests that the celebration of Confucius's birthday in Qufu and Dachuan was a rather late cultural invention. Specifically, it grew out of the attempts by the Republican regime to distinguish itself from its imperial predecessors. In a conscious attempt at identity assertion, a delegation of officials representing the new polity converged on Qufu in 1913, the second year after the founding of the republic, to celebrate Confucius's birthday anniversary. The government decreed in 1914 that the sage's birthday would be celebrated as a national holiday, with a government-financed sacrificial ceremony in Qufu. This newly created ritual was called guo ji, or "state-organized sacrificial ceremony." Before the Communist takeover of Qufu, its participants included representatives of the national government, provincial governors, and county magistrates (Kong Fanyin 1992: 185–89; Kong Zhaozeng 1934: 2, 6–7). In short, the state-sponsored worship of Confucius shifted from seasonal rites to a celebration of the sage's birthday in the Republican period.

The exact year that Dachuan adopted the birthday celebration from Qufu cannot be textually verified. Interviews suggest that it probably became a local practice around 1930, after the Kongs of Dachuan made contact with Qufu. Their response to the government-promoted celebration of the sage's birthday fits a larger historical pattern of interactions between state authorities and local elites. James Watson has described this pattern as "the process of religious standardization" (J. Watson 1985: 310). In this process, state authorities actively intervened in the local organization of religious cults. They did this by approving or outlawing the worship of certain deities and historical figures. In the approved cases, miraculous deeds reportedly performed by deities or virtues popularly attributed to great men were not only recorded but publicly proclaimed by government officials, who often went so far as to determine and register the birth and death dates of the deified (see C. K. Yang 1961: 180–217). Local elites—literate men, successful landowners, and wealthy merchants—eagerly cooperated with state authorities in the standardization of cults. Their willingness to adhere to official directives was rooted in the hope that they could thus "gentrify" themselves (J. Watson 1985: 293).

In relating this pattern of state-society interaction to the Dachuan case, one must acknowledge that the Kongs' response to a state-initiated ritual had its own peculiarities. The most important deity for the Kongs was, of course, Confucius, whose public standing declined precipitously as radical Chinese students and intellectuals began in the 1910's and 1920's to hold Confucian teachings and institutions responsible for the nation's backwardness. In 1928, in the midst of attacks on Confucianism, students at a college in Qufu staged a play ridiculing Confucius, which resulted in a bitter lawsuit that attracted nationwide attention through the news media. While the lawsuit proceeded, liberal-minded scholars and distinguished writers published opinion pieces on whether Confucius should be ridiculed. Lu Xun, perhaps the most influential writer of the day, sided with the students and compiled a collection of writings that belittled the Kong clan council. The council won the lawsuit but could not control the damaging publicity it triggered.

Adding injury to the insult suffered by the clan council in 1928–29 was the proposal of several top government officials that the Kong "ritual lands" be nationalized. The farm fields, given by successive emperors, had provided revenues for the year-round sacrificial ceremonies in Qufu and the lavish lifestyle of the Yansheng dukes and their families. Furthermore, thousands of Kongs tilling the ritual lands enjoyed tax reductions.

With the attacks by liberal intellectuals, the humiliation of the highly publicized lawsuit, and the economic threat posed by the plan to nationalize the ritual lands, the clan council was on the defensive; one strategy it developed to cope with these troubling developments was the genealogy project. Initiated in 1930, this project was essentially aimed at rallying Kongs throughout the country in support of the Kongs of Qufu. In other words, it was in the midst of a crisis that the clan council decided to break with tradition by recognizing the descent claims of the Kong diaspora. The very fact that the confiscation of ritual lands was averted by the intervention of the finance minister, himself a member of the Kong diaspora, may have bolstered the council's decision to forge alliances with Kongs outside Qufu.

These events suggest that the ceremony commemorating Confucius's birthday was introduced by Dachuan at a critical juncture in the history of the Kong clan. Dachuan's adoption of this ritual occasion and the village's involvement in the genealogy project undertaken in Qufu combined to provide legitimacy for the Kongs' claim to a sacred ancestry. Within the broader context of rapidly changing Chinese society, the genealogical recognition and the ritual ceremony that Dachuan acquired from Qufu in the 1930's were two inseparable developments.

Genealogical Knowledge and Making Historical Sense

After the Communist victory in 1949, the birthday ritual was halted. Since its revival at Dachuan in 1984, it has come to occupy a central place in ancestor worship, which used to proceed from ancestors' tombs to Dachuan's Confucius temple. Given that the older tombs had been destroyed by the damming of the Yellow River and that the ceremonies at tombs of immediate ancestors were restricted to individual households, the new birthday celebration serves as a rallying point in the reorganization of the Kong lineage, helping its recovery from decades of chaos.

The reinstated ceremony is underpinned by historically and morally explicit exegetics. In the absence of these exegetics, the purely technical aspects of the ritual performance would be meaningless in the eyes of the temple managers. This is why the ritual handbook they produced in 1991 includes texts that directly address the history of the Kongs and the legacy of Confucian ethics. The genesis of these texts can be, in part, traced to local genealogies. The central themes of the historical and moral texts in the ritual handbook are the past glory of the Kongs and the continuity of the Kong descent line. These themes become evident in the first five pages, which contain 41 poems, suitable for hanging as couplets (*dui lian*) on the temple's columns. Composed in a grand style, some poems exalt the greatness of Confucius in Chinese history whereas others laud the continuity of the Kong bloodline.

In the Kong ritual handbook, the place and time of Confucius's birth are specified in a reference to the *Records of the Grand Historian* by Sima Qian (see Chapter 2), which places the sage's birth in Nishan, near Qufu, on the twenty-seventh day of the eighth Chinese month in 551 B.C. The reference to Confucius's birth is written above a list of the sage's direct heirs over 77 generations, culminating in Kong Decheng, the Yansheng Duke now in Taiwan. Honorary titles and official ranks are appended to personal names. A few pages later is a fuller account of Confucius's contributions to Chinese culture, with emphasis on the honors he received throughout the imperial era and the relevance of his teachings to contemporary society.

The glorification of Confucius continues in other texts, including two memorial elegies and an essay on the temple's past and its reconstruction in 1991. Altogether there are seven elegies or memorial texts (*ji wen*) dedicated to Confucius, his son, his grandson, his disciples, and the six local ancestors who founded the Kong lineage in Gansu. The elegies for the local ancestors contain vivid descriptions of the migration of the Kongs from Guangdong to Gansu and then from Lanzhou to Dachuan. Each elegy concludes with a plea to the enshrined deities to accept the sacrifices offered by the liturgists. The exact words are *shang xiang*, "may you accept this," a standard expression in formal sacrificial rites (C. K. Yang 1961: 40; Ebrey 1991: 177).

In their formulation of moral, historical, and technical explanations to be included in the ritual handbook, the temple managers sought out whatever written materials might be relevant. This search was strictly limited to the Dachuan area. Because they were not affiliated with an academic institution, they did not have access to the provincial library's rare-book depository. If they had, they would have found highly useful materials there. Three complete sets of ritual texts and moral teachings on the worship of Confucius can be found in local gazetteers and other official records stored at the library.

Because of a policy discouraging public access, the temple managers of Dachuan did not resort to their county's historical archives either. My own experience in these archives illustrates the restrictions the Kongs would have faced. The first time I entered the local archives to see if there were any files on Dachuan and the Kongs, a woman librarian asked if I were related to the Kongs by blood or marriage. When I said no, she allowed me to enter a room with three large cabinets filled with index cards. When asked why being related to the Kongs would be a problem, the librarian explained that the archives contained thousands of personal files, that is, secret dossiers on individuals. Although these files had not been updated since the end of the Maoist era, their confidential nature required a careful screening of any visitors. The contents of these dossiers, compiled from reports of local police, informers, and village cadres, range from court verdicts to confidential reports on personal conversations. To use these files, one must obtain approval, as I did, from the county's Party committee.

One way to retrieve documents at this archive is to use a surname index, and the second most common surname listed in this index is Kong. The Kongs had "lots of historical problems," the librarian commented, adding that some of them might pose as researchers or hire an outsider to gain access to the archives and steal or destroy incriminating documents. The most common surname registered in the archives' files is Ma. This is shorthand for Muhammad and is the dominant surname among the Hui, or Chinese-speaking Muslims. Many of the Mas in the dossiers were implicated in the 1958 Muslim rebellion in nearby Dongxiang county (see Chapter 3), an indication that the rebellion was not limited to Dongxiang but involved Muslims in adjacent areas such as Yongjing county. Like the Kongs whose dossiers are in the archives, these Muslims had been kept under surveillance by local cadres. In every political campaign of the Maoist period, they were reinvestigated, resulting in a thick accumulation of government files.

Unable to use the provincial or local archives, the managers of Dachuan's Confucius temple turned to a source that some of them knew best—local genealogies. They studied two genealogies in particular. One was compiled at the turn of this century by Kong Xianmin (Kong Xianmin 1905), who lived in Xiaochuan, a village about ten kilometers upstream from Dachuan. The other was completed in 1989 by Kong Lingshu, who lived in a downstream village settled by Kongs displaced from Dachuan in 1961. Kong Lingshu's work was compiled on the basis of the 1905 genealogy, compiled by Kong Xianmin in Xiaochuan, and this is why the two genealogies share some very striking similarities and contain, in each case, more than 1,000 pages. Neither of them includes, however, a comprehensive ritual transcript that could have helped clarify ritual procedures. Their most important contribution to Dachuan's ritual handbook proved to be their moral messages and historical references. As an illustration, portions of the 1905 genealogy are summarized below:

CONFUCIUS AND QUFU

A number of texts on the origin of the Kong clan in Qufu trace the glory of Confucius and the privileges bestowed upon his descendants in imperial China. Essays on Confucius, biographies of distinguished clan members, historical accounts of Qufu, and descriptions of ancestral rituals in the sage's hometown are scattered throughout the genealogy.

LINEAGE REGULATIONS

The conduct of lineage members is prescribed in various rules. Some are merely collections of Confucius's sayings, excerpts from the penal code, or aphorisms from various ancestors. Others deal with sexual segregation, mourning duties, and filial obligations to parents and other senior relatives. It is specifically stipulated that criminals, sons-in-law, Buddhist monks, and illegitimate boys sired by outsiders or adopted from other surname groups cannot be included in the genealogy.

RITUAL PICTURES

Simple drawings provide guidelines for five grades of mourning dress, ceremonial clothes for sacrificial rites, and the physical arrangement of sacrificial altars, spirit tablets, and ritual utensils. Also included are poems (for temple couplets), two temple plans, memorial texts marking renovations, complimentary texts by scholar-officials, and detailed maps of ancestral tombs.

SOCIOECONOMIC DOCUMENTS

Well preserved in this genealogy are two marriage contracts and twelve land-purchase documents, a text commemorating an important ancestor who died in a clash with nearby Muslim groups, a registry of property divisions, a list of sacrificial animals, and numerous texts on the history of the local Confucius temple.

MIGRATION HISTORY

The settlement of the Kongs in the Dachuan area is recounted primarily through short biographies of early ancestors who moved from Guangdong to Lanzhou and then to Dachuan. This history of migration is replete with specific place-names such

as the Rainbow Bridge (*cai hong qiao*) outside the eastern gate
of the once-walled city of Guangzhou and the Earth-Gate Mountain near the southern entrance to the historical city of Lanzhou.
The movements of the Kongs in Yongjing county are noted with
references to Yanjiawan (the Yan family terrace), Dachuan (big
valley), Zhongzhuang (central village), Sigou (four ravines),
Xiaochuan (small valley), Baijiachuan (the Bai family valley),
and Kongshan (the Kong family hill). Personal names and, occasionally, specific dates of death appear on page after page dealing
with generational ranks and burial places.

This genealogy bears the hallmarks of a legitimating history.
It looks back to the ultimate source of the lineage—Confucius
and his hometown. In addition to the obviously impressive connection it establishes with the ancient sage, the genealogy offers
evidence of the lineage's prestige by its many enumerated generations. In chronicling the migration from Qufu to south China
and then from Guangdong to Gansu, it demonstrates the Kongs'
ability to endure over time and space. The vast distances covered
by Kong ancestors are recorded in relation to court-assigned military missions and honors bestowed by the state.

Government records confirm the Kong migration from Qufu
to Guangzhou. Two gazetteers of Guangdong, for instance, begin
their historical accounts of official positions with Kong Ji, who
in A.D. 817 became the military superintendent of Guangzhou
(Shi Deng 1871: 23, 3; 1879: 17, 2). A descendant of this high-
ranking commandant was Kong Changbi, who went to Guangdong in 900 and settled there permanently. This man, who is
regarded by the Kongs as the founding ancestor of the Kong clan's
Guangdong branch, arrived in the city of Guangzhou as a
middle-ranking officer accompanying an envoy from the central government.

Coming to Gansu

When it comes to the migration from Guangdong to Gansu,
there appears a peculiar gap in the written documents produced

by the Kongs in the Dachuan area. The 1905 genealogy, for example, claims that Kong Jiaxing, the focal ancestor of the Kongs throughout Yongjing county, arrived in Gansu from Huizhou, Guangdong province, "at the end of the Song dynasty." This assertion is elaborated upon in the 1991 ritual handbook written by the temple managers, which says that Kong Jiaxing arrived in Lanzhou "at the end of the Song dynasty and the beginning of the Ming dynasty." The ritual handbook further asserts that Kong Jiaxing distinguished himself as a heroic military officer after being "ordered by an imperial decree to march to Gansu to restore peace and to sweep away diabolic forces" (Kong Xiangguo 1991: 45). In these local records, the reference to "the end of the Song dynasty and the beginning of the Ming dynasty"—a span of more than 100 years—is extremely vague, perhaps deliberately so. The political regime between the Chinese-governed Song and Ming dynasties was the Yuan dynasty (1264–1368), which was controlled by the Mongols.

The failure even to mention the existence of the Mongol-ruled Yuan dynasty allows the depiction of the founding ancestor of the Kongs in this part of Gansu as a Han Chinese patriot, which contradicts the historical circumstances. The Han Chinese control of Lanzhou was supplanted, in 1131, by the Nuzhen army out of the northeast. After the Nuzhen forces took Lanzhou, they had to defend it in many hard-fought battles against the nearby Tibetan troops and the Xixia Kingdom (r. 1032–1227). This the Nuzhen did successfully, but they proved unequal to the military challenge of the Mongols, who captured Lanzhou in 1226. In a series of fierce battles, the Mongols then moved south, eventually conquering the city of Huizhou in 1278. It was near this last stronghold of Han Chinese resistance that Wen Tianxiang, the famed prime minister of the Song dynasty, was captured. Wen's arrest and the Mongols' destruction of the Chinese royal family the next year certainly would make 1278–79 "the end of the Song Dynasty," but it also marked the beginning of absolute control by the Mongols over China.

It was not until 1369 that Lanzhou was in the hands of Han

Chinese troops again. In other words, it took 238 years for the city to be returned to Chinese control, in this case by the Ming dynasty. By the time Lanzhou fell to the Ming, the Kongs had lived in Gansu for seven generations. A great-great-grandson of Kong Jiaxing secured a low-ranking official position two years after the Han Chinese government was installed in Lanzhou.

All of this means that Kong Jiaxing, along with his son and four nephews, arrived in Lanzhou while it was still under Mongol rule. The compiler of the 1905 genealogy and the temple managers who wrote the ritual handbook in 1991 were sorely tempted to cover up this history of implied acquiescence if not collaboration in hopes of depicting an illustrious ancestry. This they did by describing Kong Jiaxing as a decorated officer and a Han Chinese patriot sent by imperial authorities to defend a frontier region. To represent this ancestor as a Han Chinese patriot, however, they had to separate his arrival in Gansu from the Mongols' rule. This gave rise to the clumsy account that he reached Lanzhou at "the end of the Song dynasty and the beginning of the Ming dynasty."

The compilers of the 1905 genealogy and the 1991 ritual handbook were obviously less interested in establishing historical fact than in making historical sense. By deleting, evading, and distorting certain aspects of history that might not effectively enhance the reputation of their ancestry, the compilers contributed to the myth that the focal ancestor of the Kongs was not only a Han Chinese patriot, but a distinguished defender of national integrity. The temptation to camouflage certain aspects of the Kong migration to Gansu must have been great when they were unclear or unsuitable for depicting the founder of the Kong lineage in the Dachuan area.

Keepers of Genealogical Information

To appreciate further the socio-historical significance of genealogical records and especially their connections with Dachuan's Confucius temple, I should say something about three

men. The first is Kong Xianmin, who compiled the 1905 Xiaochuan genealogy with the assistance of three of his sons. The
second is Kong Qinghui, the Lanzhou merchant who brought the
Kong clan genealogy from Qufu in 1948. He was Kong Xianmin's
youngest son, and his name appears at the front of each of the
ten volumes of the 1905 genealogy. The third is Kong Xiangqian,
whose father was Kong Xianmin's eldest son and thus Kong
Qinghui's eldest brother.

Kong Xiangqian, the last of the three persons mentioned
above, was still alive when I finished my fieldwork in 1992, but
we repeatedly failed to meet each other. He spent most of his
time in the county seat and, in the summer of 1992, was taken to
a hospital in the county seat. He had developed a terrible cough,
which was diagnosed as a symptom of lung cancer. Probably
sensing that his days were numbered, he decided to leave a full
account of how the 1905 genealogy survived the Cultural Revolution, when similar records were destroyed either by rural cadres or their fearful owners. Regrettably, I was detained by other
matters and had to ask someone else to videotape his account
in the hospital.

The 1905 genealogy was passed to the eldest of Kong Xianmin's three sons, Kong Xiangqian's father, who guarded it with
great care and seldom allowed even his own family to see it. It
was locked in a hardwood box on the family's household altar.
On the rare occasions it was taken out, incense and oil burners
were first lit and the reader had to wash his hands and kowtow
before the genealogical box could be opened. When his father
died, Kong Xiangqian was entrusted with the genealogy. At the
onset of the Cultural Revolution, he received news from Lanzhou that the 108-volume clan genealogy that his uncle Kong
Qinghui brought from Qufu had been burned by Red Guards.
This prompted him to hide the 1905 genealogy in an underground storeroom in Zhongzhuang village where he lived.

There the genealogy remained until Kong Xiangqian retrieved
it in the early 1980's. He surprised many people when he turned
it over to the county archives in 1989. He did this for several

reasons, he said. The head of the county archives knew that the Kongs had kept some private records for several centuries. In particular, he had learned that Kong Xiangqian had a genealogy dating back to 1905 that contained several old land deeds. The archivist wanted to use this document to assist a local government effort to compile a new county gazetteer. He also wanted the original copy to enrich the archives' rare book collection. After a few rounds of negotiation, Kong Xiangqian surrendered the genealogy. At this time, he was a salaried cadre in the county's education bureau and the pressure on him to surrender the genealogy came from very high-ranking officials in the local bureaucracy. In exchange, Kong Xiangqian was given a photocopy of the manuscript.

One temple manager who had read both the original and the photocopied genealogy was Kong Fanjun, who, like Kong Xiangqian, lived in Zhongzhuang, a village near Dachuan. Kong Fanjun, who was 73 in 1992, had attended middle school and been trained in classical Chinese. His nickname was "big accountant"—he was about six feet tall—and had been for many years the ablest bookkeeper in his village. A generation senior to Kong Xiangqian and a respected calligrapher, Kong Fanjun had been permitted to borrow the genealogy to read at home. As one of the fourteen managers of Dachuan's Confucius temple, he applied his readings of the genealogy and his calligraphic skills to the composing of the ritual handbook. He focused on the handbook's memorial text dealing with the temple's history and most recent reconstruction.

Kong Fanjun's interest in writing the temple memorial was remarkably personal: he was trying to honor the memory of his own father. In Chapter 2, I mentioned that Dachuan's Confucius temple was burned down when Muslim soldiers broke into Dachuan in 1864. In the same year, more than 700 members of the Kong lineage died in clashes between the local Han and Muslim populations. It seems that it took the Kongs many years to recover from the devastation of 1864. It was not until 1934 that a temple complex with three great halls was rebuilt. The reconstruction project was supervised by 26 elderly and middle-aged political leaders of the Kong lineage. One of the two leading members of this group was Kong Fanjun's father, a well-to-do landowner, an accomplished calligrapher, and, by most accounts, a shrewd power broker. Kong Fanjun was barely ten when his father first took him to the construction site and to the subsequent temple ceremonies. In the late 1940's, Kong Fanjun became an assistant liturgist. In the memorial text he wrote in 1991 to commemorate the temple's most recent resurrection, he did not fail to include a passage about his father's role in the temple's reconstruction of 1934. Nor did he neglect to include his own name in the 1991 temple memorial, or to sign his name under the title of the text he composed and copied by hand. The text on the temple's history and its recent reappearance was copied onto a huge wooden plaque and hung in a prominent place on the façade of the temple's main building.

The other genealogy that proved useful to the temple managers was, to repeat myself, compiled by Kong Lingshu, who lived in the village of Huangci, 20 kilometers downstream. In 1992, on an April afternoon, I traveled to this village to meet him. After I introduced myself and expressed my wish to see the genealogy he had written, he stared at me as if he did not understand. He said I must be looking for someone else. I took out a note of introduction from one of the temple managers in Dachuan. Kong Lingshu carefully examined the note before he started to apologize. He had taken me for a government official. Why was he so afraid of officials? He explained that officials always meant trouble for him. To him I looked not just like an official, but like a city official, which, he said, was even worse. When we moved from his courtyard into his room and exchanged cigarettes, he explained why he was afraid of urban officials. Whenever well-dressed urban officials showed up in a village, he said, it meant the onset of a major political campaign. They were usually sent down from cities to help rural cadres implement new government policies, especially when such policies were expected to meet with local resistance. When I first said I wanted to see his genealogy, he was afraid I would confiscate it. This fear was not groundless.

Kong Lingshu's long-deceased father was a semiprofessional genealogist in Dachuan. He used to be well paid to help the Kongs and other family groups design and paint big charts of ancestors' names that could be hung from a house's eaves.[5] On these charts, which documented five to ten generations, the names of the dead were written in designated boxes drawn in the shape of spirit tablets.[6] Kong Lingshu's father also helped multi-family groups to update their book-sized genealogies. He was thus able to study and copy, in a selective manner, the contents of extant local genealogies. He focused on poems, mottoes, and ritual regulations. Usually, genealogies were difficult for outsiders to obtain. But since Kong Lingshu's father was considered a good genealogist and a reliable person, he was permitted to take home other families' genealogies to study and copy.

Kong Lingshu picked up his father's trade before he joined the Nationalist army. After his unit was defeated by the Communists, he returned to Dachuan, where he soon realized that he could no longer make a living by writing and copying genealogies. Still, he had inherited a large chest of genealogical histories, religious manuals, and other documents collected by his father. He told me that these texts were burned in 1967, during the Cultural Revolution, by a work team of government officials, led by an urban official. Then, starting in 1978, Kong Lingshu discovered enough customers to resume his trade, and on his own he began work on a genealogical history of the Kongs. However, the finished work lacked the charts and tables of descent needed to connect the most recent generations. Recording the dead of the past few decades would have been an impossible job for one person, given that probably more than half the 20,000 Kongs in Yongjing county were born after 1949. When urged by a few elderly Kongs to develop a complete name list, he realistically declined.

One of Kong Lingshu's contributions to Dachuan's Confucius temple was the 41 poems in the ritual handbook. These poems are designed to be copied in big characters on long sheets of paper to hang as couplets on the temple's columns. In rural China, vertical couplets on walls, gates, or columns are a feature of exterior and interior decoration for practically all residential buildings. In Dachuan, they appear at the main entrance of walled compounds, the gates of main halls, and flanking household shrines. Old couplets are replaced for weddings and funerals. During the lunar New Year, even the latrine and enclosures for domestic animals are decorated with couplets. Good couplets contain well-paced rhythms, graceful calligraphy, and appropriate meanings. As symbols of prosperity and respect for learning, they are literally the "face" of a rural household. Most local temples in Gansu have written couplets, either pasted or inscribed on wooden posts. Dachuan's Confucius temple is no exception. From its compound's arched entrance to the columns and gates of its main hall and side rooms, the paper couplets are elegantly composed and demonstrate a cultivated hand.

But if the local histories, religious manuals, and classical poems Kong Lingshu had inherited from his father were really burned during the Cultural Revolution, how did he come up with the 41 poems in the ritual handbook? Kong Lingshu at first claimed that he had memorized most of these poems, word for word, line for line. Later he admitted that other people had offered a few of the classic poems, and that he also had consulted the poems in the 1905 genealogy and other old genealogies hidden away in the Dachuan area. His reference to hidden genealogies took me by surprise.

Not long after arriving in Dachuan in 1992, I set out to look for local genealogies and was able to examine three new ones that covered five to ten generations. The older, more comprehensive genealogies, according to their owners, had all been burned during the Cultural Revolution. Kong Lingshu told me, however, that in addition to the 1905 genealogy, three other pre-1949 genealogies had survived the Cultural Revolution. Although their existence was not widely known, he knew their whereabouts primarily through his work compiling and transcribing new genealogies since the late 1970's. He was able to consult all three of these hidden genealogies while working on his own genealogy project. He copied a number of texts, including poems, from these records. One of the genealogies he consulted was in the village of Sigou (four ravines), separated from Dachuan only by a pair of railway tracks. After returning to Dachuan, I asked one of the temple managers to speak to the owner of the Sigou genealogy. The owner admitted to the genealogy's existence, but said it had been lent to an agnatic kinsman in Lanzhou a few days earlier. When asked for his kinsman's address, he said that he had forgotten it! Frustrated, I wrote to Kong Lingshu saying that I had not been able to see the Sigou genealogy and that I would like to photocopy his genealogical history. He did not respond. My request to photocopy the original at the county archives was also turned down by the archivists.

My determination to get hold of a local genealogy eventually paid off. Through several elderly men in Dachuan and the village's chief accountant, I was able to borrow the photocopied version of the 1905 genealogy. When I took it to a research institute in Lanzhou that had a Japanese photocopying machine, the accountant insisted on accompanying me. He had been told that he was responsible for returning the genealogy safely to its owner as soon as it was copied.

Genealogy and Lineage Theory

What is the reason for the extreme precautions taken to safeguard the genealogical records, the older ones of which have not been updated since they were compiled decades ago? It is likely that these records are regarded by the local people as having an intrinsic sacred value.[7] As described earlier, elderly Kongs in Dachuan would first kowtow, wash their hands, set out oil burners, and light incense before opening the book-sized genealogies or displaying the wall-sized ancestral charts.

Another possible explanation for the caution the local people demonstrated regarding genealogies is that not long before these documents had been targets of destruction. A 1991 sociological survey of fifteen Chinese villages, ten in the coastal regions and five in the interior (Wang Huning 1991: 291–581) discovered that people in twelve of these villages had possessed genealogical records from the pre-1949 period. The most comprehensive genealogy included 20 generations. All but one of these genealogies were destroyed in the 1950's and 1960's.

The most provocative and also somewhat problematic interpretation is that some aspects of local life recorded in genealogies are too sensitive to be revealed to outsiders.[8] This is because genealogical records are a quasi-legal instrument in the development of lineage organizations (Eberhard 1962; Hu 1948; Liu Hui-chen 1959; Taga 1960). In anthropological theories on Chinese kinship, lineages have been strictly defined as descent groups with substantial corporate properties and extensive agnatic networks (see, e.g., H. Baker 1977, 1979; Freedman 1966; Potter 1970: 121–38; J. Watson 1982b: 69–100; R. Watson 1985; Ebrey & J. Watson 1986). The collectively owned estates are treated as "the central feature of these lineages," which are examined by scholars primarily as property-owning organizations (Ebrey 1986: 40). Distribution of revenues from the collectively owned farm fields and access to a lineage trust fund depended on whose names were registered in the local genealogy. Among other things, this required those in charge of the lineage's account books to have a good command of genealogical knowledge (J. Watson 1975: 171). It is not surprising that much of the primary documentation that researchers use in studying ancestor halls, corporate estates, and trust funds in local communities in pre-1949 mainland China, contemporary Hong Kong, or Taiwan has come from genealogies.

Economic matters are also recorded in the genealogies produced by Kong Xianmin in 1905 and Kong Lingshu in 1989. Yet these recorded economic references are of a purely historical nature and have nothing to do with the present-day distribution of profits from collectively owned properties. The temple managers in Dachuan do indeed control the temple compound, which is a corporate domain about the size of a basketball court. Nonetheless, they have no extra land under their control. Nor do they have anything to do with the distribution of profits from the fish ponds under the collective ownership of local villagers. It is village cadres who control the fish ponds, the most important collectively held assets remaining after decollectivization.

If a genealogy can no longer be evaluated as a source of economic information, what kind of social significance does it retain? A sophisticated reply to this question can be developed by considering a recent article by Myron Cohen (1990: 509–34). Referring to a rich body of work based on fieldwork in Taiwan and Hong Kong, and on earlier research in Fujian and Guangdong provinces, Cohen explains that the basic conclusion to be drawn from research in these southern regions is that Chinese lineage organization cannot be analyzed without reference to the accumulation of substantial corporate holdings, such as ancestor halls and lineage-controlled lands or business enterprises. An important implication of this view is that well-to-do individuals within a lineage are bound to dominate its senior positions and thus its orientation in terms of ideology and social action. Relying on recent fieldwork in north China, Cohen proposes to rethink lineage theory in China anthropology by applying what he calls a "fixed genealogical mode of kinship." That is to say, the workings of patrilineal ties within a Chinese lineage could be determined by the relative seniority of descent lines. In other words, the unity of a lineage may hinge on ritual recognition of the senior descent line, whose members are represented by a succession of eldest sons from the founding ancestor. More simply, a lineage may be formed in the absence of significant corporate holdings or even without a formal ancestor hall, as long as its members acknowledge the senior descent line's genealogical position, the idea of a common ancestry, and the solidarity of patrilineal ties through tomb-site rituals and the updating of genealogies.

Returning to the Dachuan case, what defines the totality of the Kong lineage in the post-Mao era is indeed what Cohen has called "a fixed genealogical mode of kinship." More specifically, Dachuan occupies a leading position among the 23 Kong settlements in Yongjing not because of some economic advantages, but rather what we might call "genealogical heirship," in two historical senses. First, and to repeat myself, it was in Dachuan where the four founding ancestors of the Kong lineage took up residence. This means that all four segments of the Kong lineage trace their lines of descent to Dachuan. In addition, all four segments of the lineage are still represented in Dachuan today, while the same continuity cannot be claimed by the other Kong villages. Second, the four founding ancestors of the lineage died and were buried in Dachuan. Their graves once made Dachuan the magnet of tomb-site rituals that were regularly performed by each of the lineage's four major segments. As noted earlier, the tomb-site rituals were followed by a lineage-focused ceremony at Dachuan's Confucius temple. The destruction of the lineage's older tombs deprived Dachuan of its central position in the Kong tomb-site rituals, but it is still regarded as the "old settlement" (lao zhuang) by the people living in other Kong villages. This historical status enables the Kongs living in Dachuan today to claim that the Confucius temple they have rebuilt represents a joint ritual enterprise serving the lineage's four segments. We shall see in the next chapter that even when another Confucius temple was built, in 1992, in a Kong village not far from Dachuan, it was the managers of Dachuan's Confucius temple who dominated and directed the ritual proceedings at the second Confucius temple.

8

Memory of Cultural Symbols

From the Ancient City to Ritual Symbolism

In his study *La cité antique*, which first appeared in 1864, N. D. Fustel de Coulanges (1956) interpreted the religious rituals of ancient Rome in terms of what we would now call "boundary-maintaining mechanisms" (Munn 1973: 582). A case in point is the altar in every Roman household on which a few coals were kept constantly burning as a symbol of family continuity. The foundations for an anthropology of symbolism were laid around the turn of this century when other scholars, such as Robertson Smith ([1889] 1956), Arnold van Gennep ([1908] 1960), and Emile Durkheim ([1911] 1954) also began analyzing rituals in light of "a cluster of sacred symbols" (Geertz 1957: 424) that reveals a given society's cosmological views and social solidarity.

In this chapter, ritual symbolism will be analyzed in terms of how subject it is to negotiation. This approach reflects a central theme in contemporary anthropology. For example, Victor Turner (1961, 1962, 1974, 1979) has stressed that ritual symbolism embodies varying degrees of "multivocality," i.e., it speaks in more than one voice. In the following pages, the multivocality of a single ritual event will be examined in detail.

As mentioned at the end of Chapter 7, another Confucius temple was opened in 1992 in a Kong village adjoining Dachuan. The village is Xiaochuan; nearly 95 percent of its male residents are surnamed Kong. Xiaochuan was settled in 1585 by a group of people who belonged to the third segment of the Kong lineage based in Dachuan. In interviews conducted in 1992, people in their seventies said that Xiaochuan also used to have an ancestral-Confucius temple. It mainly catered to the members of the lineage's third segment living in Xiaochuan. Though nobody could now recall the early history of Xiaochuan's temple, it was recalled without difficulty that Xiaochuan's temple was shut down in 1958 and was torn down three years later because it stood in the path of a railway line that was under construction. When Dachuan's Confucius temple was rebuilt in 1991, the Kongs in Xiaochuan decided it was time to reconstruct their own temple. The main structure was completed in August 1992, on a hill behind the village.

The appearance of two Confucius temples within a year triggered several remarkable changes in the Kong practice of ancestor worship. The most noticeable was the invention of a public festival to mark Confucius's birthday. The festival was an invention because it merged what traditionally had been an exclusively Kong activity of worshiping their own ancestors with a commemorative event open to the wider public. It marked a transition from exclusion to inclusion, from a lineage-based ceremony to a popular public event. The festival was first held at Dachuan in 1991 and then at Xiaochuan in 1992; it was open not only to the Kongs but to villagers bearing other surnames and even to total strangers from distant communities.

The ethnographic data presented below describe the festival's two-tier ritual order. The first tier will be called the "dominant ritual structure" and described in terms of five prescribed ritual components of the festival: space, time, objects, words, and acts. The use of these five ritual components was fixed in advance and rehearsed by the festival organizers. The second tier is the "variant ritual structure," comprising the various responses of the festival participants to the five prescribed ritual elements.

The most conspicuous of these responses was a spontaneous display of devotional acts that digressed from the dominant ritual order.

Ritual Authority and Ceremonial Rules

The primary directors of the 1992 festival were seven men, all more than 60 years old. Four were from Xiaochuan, two from Dachuan, and one from Zhongzhuang. The first four men had been chiefly responsible for the reconstruction of Xiaochuan's Confucius temple. They were in charge of every aspect of the festival except the ritual performance, which featured a lengthy nighttime ceremony and a daytime service. Thus, the leading liturgists in this religious festival were the three men from Dachuan and Zhongzhuang, all of whom were managers of Dachuan's Confucius temple. This ritual leadership reflects Dachuan's historical position as the original settlement of the Kong lineage in the area. Even during the festival, the leading liturgists from Dachuan kept telling Xiaochuan Kongs that historically theirs was a branch temple serving only one segment of the lineage, whereas Dachuan's temple was the main temple serving all four of the lineage's segments. In private, they referred to the Xiaochuan temple as a "minor temple," though it was no smaller than the one in Dachuan. In fact, it surpassed the latter in at least one physical aspect: it contained a larger-than-life-sized statue of Confucius. The significance of this statue will be explained later; first, a discussion of the festival's double liturgy.

The decision to stage both nighttime and daytime ceremonies grew out of the dilemma inherent in the merging of an ancestor ceremony with a public festival. In combining a lineage-focused activity with a public event, the festival organizers were faced with a dilemma over two rules of avoidance associated with Chinese ancestor worship.

The first rule of avoidance concerns the relationship between descendants and nondescendants. J. J. M. De Groot, a pioneer in the study of Chinese religion, wrote in the 1890's about the prevalent taboo against receiving ritual offerings from outsiders for the worship of one's own ancestors. The taboo also applied to contributing to ancestral sacrifices prepared by other descent groups. "Anything a child possesses belongs to his parents, even though they are dead," De Groot noted, adding that "offerings presented to a strange soul are regarded as a theft from the holy ones" (De Groot 1892: 1, 15). In line with De Groot, Hugh Baker says: "Other people's dead were of little concern: the only dead to be worshipped were one's own dead, one's ancestors" (H. Baker 1979: 75). It is interesting that Baker buttresses his statement by saying that "to sacrifice to ancestors not one's own is presumptuous," an aphorism attributed to Confucius in *lun yu, The Analects* (1979: 75).

The second rule of avoidance concerns the relationship between men and women. Chinese women play an active role in death rituals and graveside ceremonies (Ahern 1975: 269–90; J. Watson 1982a: 155–85). Especially in places where the custom is to display ancestor tablets at domestic altars year round, Chinese women assisted their husband or father in caring for the immediate ancestors. Ceremonies performed in lineage-controlled ancestor halls, by contrast, are dominated by men. Wives and daughters are rarely if ever allowed to take part in such proceedings out of fear that their ritually unclean condition might defile the proceedings (Freedman 1958: 85–86; H. Baker 1979: 94).

Were the festival's organizers and senior liturgists aware of these rules? In their own accounts, they claimed that such rules were followed by other descent groups in Yongjing, but that the Kong lineage was an exception. Even in the pre-Communist era, they said, outsiders and women had never been denied access to the Kong ancestor rites. They spoke of the open-mindedness of their forebears in having regularly invited outsiders to join the temple-based Kong ancestor rites. An interesting bit of history emerged in interviews with elderly people of both sexes. To minimize the influence of hearsay, the interviews focused on eye-witness accounts of the sacrificial rites at Dachuan's Confucius temple in the 1930's and 1940's.

According to these accounts, women, especially elderly women married to Kongs, were permitted to enter the temple compound to observe the ceremony while it was being con-ducted by lineage elders inside the temple's central hall. Only after the ceremony was completed, however, could women enter the hall to kowtow and burn incense. This was, then, a limited form of female participation.

As for the outsiders invited to Kong ceremonies, they tended to be local officials, well-educated villagers, and successful busi-nessmen. In the name of worshiping Confucius, the lineage in-vited these prominent outsiders to the sacrificial rites and a post-ceremonial feast. Generally, one of these guests would deliver the ceremony's opening speech, praising the Kongs for their faith in Confucius and devotion to their founding ancestors. These elite outsiders joined the lineage elders in the sacrificial rites inside the offering hall, but they kowtowed only to the spirit tablet of Confucius.

Given the circumscribed form of female participation and the selective involvement of outsiders, it appears that the Kong lin-eage in the past had bent, but not completely ignored, the rules of avoidance for participation in ancestor worship. At Dachuan's provisional ancestor shrine, in use from 1985 to 1990, the Kongs resumed the practice of inviting selected outsiders and allowing women into the shrine to kowtow and burn incense after the sacrifices had been offered.

From Restriction to Compromise

The situation was quite different at the newly opened tem-ples. Participation by outsiders was no longer restricted. Nor were women barred while the sacrifices were being offered. In the afternoon before the 1992 nighttime ceremony in Xiao-chuan, a procession carrying the sacrificial offerings to the temple was staged. The procession set off from a residential court-yard, following a speech by a Mr. Zhang, former head of the county's Cultural Activity Center, to open the festival. He kow-towed and offered incense to the sacrificial offerings displayed on a table. After the offerings were brought to the temple, the participants were asked to come back for the following day's day-time service.

The intervening night's ceremony was supposed to be at-tended by a select group of men, most of them both elderly and prominent, from the Kong lineage. The selection began with let-ters of invitation from the Xiaochuan festival organizers to a number of respected elderly men in the Kong villages of Yongjing county. In consultation with other key members of their com-munities, these elders chose the final candidates. During the nighttime ceremony, which began at midnight and continued until sunrise, about eighty representatives of the Kong lineage took turns kowtowing. A flute, a drum, and an *erhu* (a two-stringed instrument) provided music at intervals in the ritual. Four separate rites were performed. The first featured the chant-ing of a written plea calling down the ancestors' spirits to the temple to enjoy the sacrifices. In the closing rite, known locally as "seeing off the spirits" (*song shen*), everyone was asked to kneel with bowed head to show respect while the spirits de-parted the temple.

Although the senior liturgists from Dachuan's Confucius temple stressed during preparations for the nighttime ceremony that it was only for select members of the lineage, they knew from their experience the previous year that other people proba-bly would try to enter the temple's main hall. Their anxiety about possible violations of the nighttime ceremony was tempo-rarily eased by a heavy downpour that started shortly before the ceremony was to begin. They assumed that not so many people would show up after all, since the heavy rain had turned the steep trails leading up to the temple into dangerously slippery paths. When they arrived at the temple, however, they noticed that in addition to the invited Kong representatives, a large crowd had reached the temple compound. These people sought shelter from the rain under two canvas tents that had been set up in the compound for the next day's ceremony and feast. After a brief consultation among the senior liturgists from Dachuan and the festival organizers from Xiaochuan, all three doors of the temple's main hall were opened to allow the crowd to watch the ceremony. Older women were allowed to sit on the floor in two peripheral areas inside the hall.

The ceremony proceeded in nearly perfect order, even though the temple hall was packed with people. The rites were conducted with precision and solemnity even though the assistants to the senior liturgists did not completely understand the chanted texts or every term for ceremonial objects. The assistants' primary responsibilities were to transfer the sacrificial meat and to arrange ritual objects such as candles, oil-burners, and sacrificial wine.

The Kong ritual language posed even greater difficulties for many of the men selected to participate in the ceremony. These men's chief duty was to kowtow and offer incense according to the instructions of the senior liturgists—simple tasks had they all understood the ritual language. To aid them, a script had been prepared in simple Chinese. Whenever the ritual performers were confused about a particular term or a directive calling for a specific ritual act, they were assisted by a schoolteacher who held the script. With the script as guide, the teacher used everyday terms to prompt the ritual performers on what to do and which ritual objects to pick up.

Some of the selected participants did not even know the ritual words for candles or incense. The translation of ritual language into cues in plain Chinese caused remarkably little disruption. Whenever it was necessary to resort to the script, the schoolteacher whispered discreetly. Amid the loudly disclaimed ritual speeches and instructions, he paraphrased the more difficult expressions in a hushed voice, almost as if he feared disturbing the enshrined spirits.

The women allowed into the hall had even less sense of what

the senior liturgists were saying. Yet they showed extraordinary patience and intently observed each ritual act the men performed. Several elderly women who had married into the Kong lineage and held senior generational rank were given a special opportunity to join the men during one of the rites. At the ceremony's end, all the spectators kowtowed inside the temple hall.

Most of the women who attended the nighttime ceremony were Kong daughters who had married into other villages or women who had married into the Kong lineage. A significant number of women, however, had no relation to the Kong lineage. One was a shaman from a non-Kong village about twenty kilometers from Xiaochuan, who came to the ceremony with more than thirty women from her hometown. Her group carried a silk banner with four large Chinese characters—*xing ru sheng shi*, literally, "Now is a Great Era for Upholding Confucianism." Along the edge, in smaller characters, were the women's names and the address of their village. None was surnamed Kong or related to the Kongs by marriage. All the characters on the banner were written in the traditional Chinese script.

Ritual Objects and Religious Ideas

Unlike the temple in Dachuan, the one erected in Xioachuan had an impressive, larger-than-life-sized statue of Confucius. Molded in clay and painted in bright colors, the statue was unveiled prior to the midnight ceremony. In having the statue made, the Kongs did three things that attracted much attention in Yongjing county. First, the statue was more than three meters high, taller than any other religious statues in Yongjing except the towering stone figures of Binglingsi, an ancient Buddhist pilgrimage site and a government-run tourist attraction. The statues in Binglingsi were carved centuries ago on cliffs and in mountain caves.

Second, the Kongs in Xiaochuan hired, in 1992, a well-known craftsman and two of his apprentices to make the statue. This craftsman had specialized in the production of religious statues since a temple-building craze began to sweep through Yongjing in the early 1980's (see Chapter 9). He was highly regarded for the statues he had made for major sacred sites where temples already had reopened.

Third, the statue's appearance and internal structure were the subjects of intense deliberation. Neither the master craftsman nor any of the Kongs knew what a statue of Confucius should look like. A color photo of the Confucius statue in Qufu was cut out of a magazine to serve as a model. The question of what should be inside the statue was resolved by falling back on a local custom regarding statues of supernatural beings. According to this custom, a statue's internal parts must approximate the anatomy of a real person in order to activate the deity's ability to respond to human supplications. Thus a ruby and artificial pearls were installed in the statue of Confucius to represent his heart and intestines. The spine was a pole fashioned from a pine tree, the arteries were made of red threads, and the kidneys and liver were constructed with silk bags containing twelve traditional medicinal herbs.

News of the renowned craftsman's arrival and the statue's unusual size provoked interest throughout Yongjing. The Kongs' refusal to disclose how much the statue cost or what items were secreted inside gave rise to the widely circulated rumor that it contained gold, real pearls, and many rare gemstones. This rumor fueled a burning curiosity about the statue, and was a reason why outsiders from about forty villages came to the festival.

The statue had the effect of "de-ancestralizing" Confucius. The local people had never heard of making statues of ancestors. What religious statues they had seen depicted nonancestral deities in Buddhist monasteries, Taoist temples, and community shrines.[1] In the local view, a statue designed for worship had to be the effigy of a god or goddess who could protect everyone, irrespective of family origin or social background. By making a statue of Confucius, the Kongs unwittingly transposed their ancestor into the realm of nonancestral gods. The statue immediately assumed popular associations with the clay figures in Buddhist, Taoist, and local-gods temples. While the Kongs themselves continued to regard Confucius as their ancestor, outsiders treated him, as we shall see, like a deity who could be worshiped by all and who had to respond to appeals from the general population for protection and good fortune. One way to appreciate the significance of this statue is to examine the arrangement of two altars for offerings during the 1992 festival.

One Statue and Two Offering Tables

The statue of Confucius occupied the central position in the main hall, flanked by four spirit tablets dedicated to the 76 Confucian disciples and six founders of the Kong lineage. In front of the statue was a wooden altar displaying the most important offerings—the head of a pig, an entire sheep, a chicken, and a rabbit, all uncooked. These sacrifices were surrounded by small slices of cooked pork and other foods. They were arranged in advance by the festival organizers, and were watched over by four middle-aged men. The meat was to be distributed later among the festival organizers and their assistants. Some of it was to be eaten at a banquet attended by elders from other Kong villages, who would then decide where and how the next year's festival should be organized.

During the daytime service, women, children, and outsiders entered the temple hall briefly to kowtow before the statue of Confucius. Kongs also kowtowed to the ancestor tablets enshrined in the hall. Those who lingered to meditate and pray were advised to go back outside to the temple courtyard, where another altar had been constructed of piled bricks. The outdoor altar differed from the one inside the temple hall in several respects. A fire was set in front of it, and it was watched over by a man and two women. There was no sacrificial meat on it; rather, it held fruit, candies, biscuits, bread, and liquor. These offerings were steadily piled up on the altar by visitors, not arranged in advance by the festival organizers. From time to time, the outer altar's caretakers distributed offerings to the crowd. Some ate the handouts, but most wrapped them up to take home.

In a sense, the temple visitors were engaging in an exchange of food at the outdoor altar, albeit an unequal trade of ordinary food for consecrated offerings. By consecrated offerings, I refer to the popular belief that food from a sacred site is blessed and possessed of beneficial properties. Several people who were interviewed that day said they were saving the food to give to children, to help them grow up strong, or to the sick, to help them regain their health.

The highlight of the daytime service was a ceremony which concluded with a senior liturgist instructing the entire crowd to fall to their knees and kowtow while a wooden plaque with the temple's name was raised and nailed above the temple hall's main entrance. Aside from this ceremony, the senior liturgists attended only to "invited guests," escorting them to the inside altar to kowtow and providing them with incense and yellow paper to burn. I will explain shortly who the "invited guests" were.

Throughout the day, the outer altar was the center of activity, thronged by visitors hoping to receive food offerings, to light tiny oil lamps and handfuls of incense, or to kneel and pray. One trait these people had in common was a hunger for ritual expression. This was especially true of the older women. Some of them knelt at the altar for as long as an hour, praying for grandsons or other good fortune and pledging to return to present offerings at the temple should their supplications be granted. A middle-aged woman came to pray for the welfare of her recently deceased son in the other world. Despite warnings by the festival organizers not to burn funeral money lest the celebration of Confucius's birthday take on the semblance of a death ritual, this woman threw a thick stack of ceremonial money into the fire and chanted songs of lamentation. She engaged in these acts of mourning for about forty minutes and then slowly made her way to a table, presided over by three men who recorded donations, to offer ten yuan to the temple.

Although the burning of funeral money and singing of lamentations associated with graveside rites were tolerated, other proscribed activities were not. An older woman whose vivid renditions of songs from *qin qiang*, or Shaanxi opera,[2] attracted a thick circle of spectators was led away by men in charge of the festival's security. Another circle formed around a middle-aged woman whose body jerked spasmodically and who mumbled what sounded like poems as if in a trance. She was carried away by the security guards, who were young men from Xiaochuan. After these women calmed down, they were sternly lectured by the festival organizers for having performed "superstitious" acts that could draw unwelcome attention from the local government to Xiaochuan's festival. Meanwhile, a group of women who lined up on the stone steps of the temple's main hall to have their photo taken were reprimanded by a sullen security guard who objected to women posing in front of the temple. When asked, none of these people could or would explain why this was forbidden for women while men were having their pictures taken with the temple as a backdrop (though never near the Confucius statue inside the temple hall).

People Ranked, Food Divided

The temple festival lasted from early morning to late afternoon, attracting about 10,000 people in the course of the day, according to the kitchen workers who provided refreshments. In addition to performing devotional acts near the inner and outside altars, many visitors sat under the canvas tents and temple eaves to partake in a feast.

To provide the food for this feast, one very large pig and six sheep were slaughtered, six large sacks of potatoes were chopped and stir-fried, and 500 kilograms of wheat flour were used to make steamed buns and deep-fried bread shaped like fish. By the accounts of the cooking staff and festival organizers, at least 2,500 people took part in the feast. In return, the diners donated more than 5,000 yuan and a wide range of goods, including costly silk coverlets and satin sheets, and pledged timber and bricks to construct extensions to the temple. According to frequent temple-goers in the crowd, this festival was among the largest religious events and public feasts in Yongjing's recent history.

In terms of the number of dishes served, the feast prepared by the temple kitchen, located in a side room, was modest. There were three main dishes: pork with mixed vegetables, mutton with scallions, and potato slices stir-fried with lard. These were a special treat, since the local diet contained little meat except during the lunar New Year holiday. Each diner also received cups of tea with rock sugar, sunflower seeds, steamed bread, and deep-fried dough strips. No alcohol was provided. A few people, including two older women, were seen carrying in bottles of clear spirits, which they shared with friends of the same sex.

The dishes were served according to a hierarchical ordering of participants. The pork and mutton dishes were offered to the "invited guests" (*xia tiao zi de*), those who had received special letters of invitation to the festival. These people tended to be the temple's major donors, the lineage's most prominent members, urban job holders, and relatives working in government offices. They included, in addition to the Mr. Zhang mentioned earlier, a deputy chairman of the Yongjing County People's Congress and a middle-ranking official of the Lanzhou city government. The former was a Kong, the latter was related by marriage.

The mutton and potato dishes were presented to the "gift-giving guests" (*dai li de*), who brought valuable presents or donated substantial amounts of money to the temple on the day of the festival. Before they were seated, the gift-giving guests, like the first category of diners, were escorted by a senior liturgist or festival organizer into the temple hall to kowtow and burn incense. Among the gift-giving guests were visitors from Lanzhou, either surnamed Kong or married to Kongs, who were working in the provincial capital. Also conspicuous among the gift-giving guests were several rural businessmen who were not related to the Kongs but were on good terms with the festival organizers.

Those who contributed smaller sums of money or less valuable gifts were called "ritual-attending guests" (gan hui de). In most cases, they were served the potato dish, supplemented with tea, bread, and in some cases fruit. Those visitors who donated insignificant amounts of money or nothing at all were called pu tong qun zhong, literally, "ordinary masses." They were offered candies, tea, and cigarettes. It was difficult to determine exactly what relationship these last two categories of people had to Xiaochuan; many of them were unknown to the festival organizers.

The three main dishes and other refreshments were served in four clearly ranked eating zones. The terrace under the temple hall's eaves was reserved for the invited guests and gift-giving visitors. Looking south from the temple, men occupied the east or left side, while the west or right side was occupied by elderly women. The two canvas tents in the temple courtyard were for the ritual guests and ordinary masses, the tent on the left for men and the one on the right for women. Tables and stools were arranged in these tents for eating, drinking tea, and chatting. The eating zones were clearly divided by gender, donation, and status.

In contrast to the chaotic scene around the outdoor altar, the diners in the four eating zones evidently understood what dishes they were entitled to and where they should sit. As one festival organizer put it: "When it comes to burning incense, people are muddle-headed. When it comes to eating, they become perfectly clear-minded." Perhaps the former situation could be characterized as "ritual disarray" and the latter as "dietary rationality." I resort to this somewhat exaggerated dichotomy only to suggest that the participants' perceptions of the festival's ritual activity were not as uniform and clear as their attitudes toward the symbolism of banquet food.

Memory and Symbolism

How does this temple festival fit the picture drawn by the general literature on Chinese temple cults and public banquets? The common view is based on earlier research in China and more recent fieldwork in Hong Kong and Taiwan. It holds that temple activities in honor of nonancestral deities function as a system of *inclusion* and provide "a collective symbol that would transcend the divergence of economic interests, class status, and social background, so as to make it possible to coalesce a large multitude into a community" (C. K. Yang 1961: 81; see also Diamond 1969: 77–80; Pasternak 1972: 111–12). An equally common but contrary view is that ancestor worship, together with its related offering of sacrifices and the sharing of banquet meals in lineage halls, amounts to a ritualized display of internal unity and thus operates as a system of *exclusion* against outsiders (see H. Baker 1979: 71–101; Freedom 1958: 81–91; J. Watson 1987: 389–401).

Neither of these views neatly applies to the festival organized by the Kongs, in part because the festival involved such mixed perceptions of the rituals' significance and in part because it merged elements of ancestor worship with a public event of religious commemoration. The festival's organizers and senior liturgists evidently tried to define and enforce the boundaries of ritual time and space, but without complete success. The essence of the festival, as I suggested at the beginning of this chapter, is best situated at the interface of social memory and ritual symbolism. The distinction drawn by scholars between popular cults and ancestor worship is certainly helpful, but it must be applied with caution and creativity. To illustrate this point, I return to the chaotic scene around the outdoor altar.

When a woman began singing Shaanxi opera songs near the outside altar, she was led away and criticized by the festival organizers for performing a "superstitious" act. The woman's eviction displeased some visitors, since singing is perfectly acceptable behavior at many temple activities. This incident thus indicates a clash between two different perceptions of the festival.

The Kongs were not unlike other Gansu villagers in their fondness for combining opera singing and the worship of local deities. In fact, two of the senior liturgists had been amateur opera performers in their youth. One had even been a locally renowned female impersonator, who maintained a passionate enthusiasm for Shaanxi opera. But these liturgists rejected the idea of singing opera as a proper form of ritual conduct during a service for ancestor worship. Although it had been stated publicly that the festival was no longer to be an exclusively Kong gathering, this did not alter the unspoken belief of the festival's organizers and liturgists that the event was primarily a Kong ritual of ancestor worship. That is why one of the liturgists privately stated that opera singing was "too cheerful" and contrary to Confucius's pronouncements on the solemnity of ancestral rites. But this does not explain why ancestors, unlike other deities, should not be entertained with opera.

The Kongs' antipathy to opera as part of their festival can be traced back to an unfortunate experience in the early 1940's. According to several elderly villagers, a Xiaochuan man who had left town to engage in business returned to Xiaochuan for an extended visit after a bumper autumn harvest. To celebrate the harvest, the businessman hired at his own expense a professional opera troupe to perform inside Xiaochuan's Confucius temple. This plan divided community leaders. Those objecting insisted that the temple was a site for solemn ancestor worship, not a stage for the vulgar jokes and sexual innuendo found in many operas. This argument was fueled by resentment of a very rich man's behaving like a patron of the entire community and using the opera for a self-serving public display of wealth and generosity.

Despite the disagreement, operas were staged at the temple. Shortly after the performances, Xiaochuan, Dachuan, and neighboring villages were hit by a severe drought—a frequent enough phenomenon in this part of Gansu, but in this case attributed to the controversial opera performances. The organizers and senior liturgists of the 1992 festival, witnessing opera singing in their midst, were reminded of the divine penalties attached to similar performances in the 1940's. Yet many, perhaps most, of the festival's participants could not have been aware of what had happened at the temple decades earlier. As outsiders, affinal relatives, villagers with mixed surnames, younger people, older women from other descent groups, and middle-aged wives married into the Kong lineage, they could hardly understand why someone would be forced to leave for singing opera. For them, singing at a sacred site was not inappropriate. In fact, in this part of China an important way to venerate deities was the very act of singing. In my trips to observe pilgrims at four sacred sites in Gansu, I noticed that women, particularly those middle-aged and older, often sang during their temple visits. The lyrics were taken from *shan shu*, "morality books," consisting of verses on the importance of religious devotion and good conduct, with much emphasis on the certainty of karmic retribution and the prospects of a better life in the next incarnation. In one temple festival at a holy mountain in Guyuan county, Ningxia, a government-financed troupe was bribed by the festival's organizers to perform Shaanxi opera to entertain the gods, attract pilgrims, and lure customers to a simultaneously organized market. The performances lasted for three days and attracted thousands of viewers.[3]

The Logic of Contradictions

It may be wise not to interpret the eviction of the woman singer at Xiaochuan as a brute expression of sexual bias or social domination. What it clearly exemplifies are the conflicting ideas and interpretations of the meaning of the Kong festival. This accounts for much of the contrast between what has been described earlier as the "dominant ritual structure" and a "variant ritual structure." Analyzing this dual ritual structure merely in terms of male dominance or fixed statue-sets would have missed the complexity of the festival's multiple dimensions of meaning. In the dominant ritual structure, five elements of ritual were manipulated by the festival organizers: time, space, language, objects, and bodily behavior. The manipulation of time involved the division of the rituals into a nighttime ceremony and day-time service intended to mark inclusion and exclusion with respect to gender, descent, and status. Ritual space and objects were arranged with similar boundaries during the festival and public feast, by the symbolic separation of the inner and outer altars. The sacrificial meat on the inner altar was offered in advance by a group of men chosen to represent the Kong lineage, while the outer altar was meant to receive food offerings from the general population regardless of gender, descent, or status differences. As for a specific ritual object, the outward appearance of the Confucius statue was modeled after the one in Qufu. But its internal features were constructed in accord with the local custom used in making statues for popular deities. Finally, the bodily movements and ritual language were established in advance and refined in rehearsal, based on the prior practice of ancestor worship.

Despite preparations and rehearsals, we discover in all these cases that the meaning of ritual and religious objects was perceived variously, altered, used in transformative ways, and even commented upon in voices that diverged from the perspectives of the festival organizers and senior liturgists. I do not mean to suggest that attitudes of the festival leaders were completely at odds with those of the participants. Had that been the case, we could hardly explain the various compromises they made, such as allowing women and outsiders into the temple hall during the nighttime ceremony and their tolerance of burning funeral money and even the singing of laments. What we have here are complex interactions between a fixed ritual order and a counterorder. The latter, as I have tried to make clear, does not imply total negativity or denial. Rather, it reflects on-site negotiations over the meaning of a newly invented festival that combined a descent-focused activity with a ritual ceremony open to the wider public. Such negotiations were precipitated by variations in historical experience, personal memory, understanding of religious symbols, and concepts of ritual propriety.

9

Finding Memories in Gansu

Memory, Politics, and Culture

In an ethnography of the Kongs, one could take a synchronic approach, a type of analysis typical of the structural functionalists and French structuralists, that treats a society as if it were "outside of time," that is, without reference to historical context. Such an approach would involve analyzing the data collected by an ethnographer in a way which assumes that the material gathered within the period of fieldwork represents largely unchanging patterns of social life of long duration.

However, a diachronic study "inside of time," that is, within a historical context, works better in the analysis of the Dachuan case, primarily because the Kongs constantly examine the meaning of their own lives and the Confucius temple's significance through a historical lens. They have tried to make sense of the temple's history and that of their community, not only by thinking about it but by actively recording it, passing down oral accounts over generations, producing extensive written genealogies, inscribing temple ornaments, writing commemorative plaques, making spirit tablets, and performing religious rituals of commemoration. These engagements help reproduce "a type of historical consciousness," to quote Steven Sangren, which is

163

"as pivotal as the historiography" once developed in China by scholar-officials (1987: 9).

What Sangren calls historical consciousness is essentially derived from the social construction of memory. In Dachuan, notions of history are inextricably intertwined with and affected by national politics, local conflict, moral reasoning, communal suffering, religious faith, and ritual undertakings. In this final chapter, I recapitulate the two main themes of this study—collective trauma and communal recovery—by focusing on the political and religious dimensions of remembrance.

Memory of Suffering

In his study of how catastrophes are portrayed in Jewish literature, Alan Mintz declares: "The Holocaust, like any historical event, has no meaning of its own to divulge. Its meaning, instead of being a discoverable essence, depends upon the interpretive traditions of the community or culture seeking that meaning" (1984: ix). He then identifies theodicy, death images, forms of lamentation, and concepts of destruction and salvation in Jewish sacred writings as an interpretive tradition vital for "creative survival." This tradition, says Mintz, constitutes the only paradigm of meaning available to Jewish survivors after the terrible injuries to body and mind inflicted by the Holocaust.

The Jewish experience dealing with cataclysmic ordeals offers important clues to the way a family-centered religion and a commitment to national identity can serve as useful mechanisms for coping with pain. In fact, Jewish cultural unity has been molded by a long historical process in which memories of old sufferings have been constantly rehearsed and ritualized. A case in point is Lucette Valensi's study (1986) of the numerous and massive calamities remembered in the Jewish community of Jerba, Tunisia, and among North African Jews who emigrated to France. By examining the popular versions of Jewish history, Valensi points out that what is remembered falls into two categories: episodes illustrating the cruelty of enemies and those showing the liberation of Jews by divine intervention. Binding these episodes together is the expectation of the coming of the Messiah (1986: 283–303). Thus it is reasonable to conclude that a society's interpretive traditions may be crucial to its capacity to deal with suffering.

Nonetheless, collective suffering cannot always be handled on the basis of time-worn models of historical interpretation. Turning memories of suffering into a source of cultural revitalization is an extremely difficult task. In a sensitive ethnography describing the removal of an Ojibwa community to a new, alien, and polluted reserve in Canada, Anastasia Shkilnyk (1985) reports that members of this community have a quite unified memory of what caused the destruction of their homeland. There is also a pervasive agreement that on the old reserve life was characterized by close family ties, communal support, moral principles, and traditional norms of social and sexual interactions. But such memories only serve to accentuate the agony of a deeply wounded culture; they provide scant defense against increasing rates of child abuse, alcoholism, divorce, suicide, gang rape, and murder (1985: 11–53, 58–63). While this deplorable situation is related to the internal decay of the traditional social order that followed resettlement, it is exacerbated by external forces of racial hostility, bureaucratic indifference, job discrimination, cultural stereotypes, and a long history of defeats since the greater Ojibwa community's initial encounter with Europeans (1985: 109–32). In contrast to the Jewish experience, what we see in the Ojibwa case is that collective memory and communal mourning do not suffice to turn pain into any positive energy; what remains is full-blown despair.

My purpose in citing the work of Mintz, Valensi, and Shkilnyk is to show that the healing of a wounded culture may depend on the collective determination not to forget, but the memory of suffering also may have a critical impact following upon those misfortunes that already have occurred. In the case of Dachuan, a community of suffering throughout the Maoist era, we can identify the traumas that were experienced by the Kongs under three headings. From the perspective of physical suffering, injuries were inflicted directly on the villagers' bodies, resulting in starvation, compulsory resettlement, forced labor, imprisonment, and in many cases death. In social terms, an effective source of practical assistance and emotional support was undermined by political assaults against religion, lineage organization, and traditional perceptions of moral authority.

Mental pain, already excruciating in the aftermath of physical injuries and communal setbacks, was intensified when the very idea of descent from Confucius, which for centuries had provided the Kongs with self-respect and community identity, became almost a mark of criminality. Although many other local groups suffered in the Maoist era, the Kongs of Dachuan were singled out for special attacks on more than one occasion. In the local Communist government's drive to establish its authority in the early 1950's, Dachuan experienced a round of revolutionary terror because of its reputation as the headquarters of the multivillage Kong lineage and as the pacesetter for the county's major religious societies. During the 1974 campaign against Lin Biao and Confucius, public rallies, big-character posters, and the ritual of humiliation that was staged at the ruins of Dachuan's Confucius temple further undermined the Kongs' morale.

On top of all this, not a household in Dachuan was spared the trauma of the village's resettlement, enforced by the local government during the centrally planned construction of the Yanguoxia hydrostation. Resettlement worsened a devastating famine, led to the loss of fertile farmland, and caused the massive destruction of family tombs. As one villager put it in 1992: "After that [resettlement], people were merely trying to survive. The village cadres tried everything to revive life and production, but people's hearts could not be pulled together anymore."

It was not only reservoir resettlement or political assaults from outside that made Dachuan a community of suffering. As symbolized by the fate of its old Confucius temple, misfortunes were internally aggravated. Furthermore, misfortunes were experienced differently by people occupying different places in an

intricate and stratified microcosm. Some were routinely victimized, as seen in the case of the so-called four bad elements who
were required to work in the "labor-reform squad." Other
people, especially the village's old Party secretary and his associates who dominated Dachuan for more than two decades, were
constantly privileged. There were also those who had previously
enjoyed prominence but were then disgraced, fired from official
positions, politically persecuted, or publicly humiliated. More
people, in fact the majority of Dachuan's residents, suffered under the burden of internal problems and disruptions from
without.

Given such circumstances, memories of the recent past in Dachuan contain some highly explosive energies. As shown in my
account of the downfall of Dachuan's former Party secretary,
memories of suffering can be grounded in internal contexts that
beget revenge. One could even argue that the village's former
Party boss was in a sense renounced as part of the local commemoration of personal and collective suffering. In a community where his authority had been rarely challenged in the Maoist era, he began to lose his local power base in the early 1980's.
By taking a noncommittal attitude toward the village's demand
for state compensation, he distanced himself in 1985 from the
Dachuan-organized sit-in at the township government building
and the demonstration at the county government compound. Instead of rewarding him for playing no part in these events, a reshuffled township government decided to appease Dachuan by
acquiescing in the local demand that he be replaced. In a symbolic move initiated by the new village cadres and approved by
higher authorities, he was fined for violating the central government's birth-limitation policy. The fine itself was a relatively
small amount, but it signified a fundamental change in Dachuan's structure of power.

The downfall of Dachuan's former Party secretary did not involve physical assault, but it still is suggestive of revenge, which
in Chinese culture forms "a way of honoring the commitments
that constitute one's social identity" (Madsen 1990: 179), espe-

cially when it is motivated by obligations to one's family, kinsmen, political allies, and personal friends.

   In specific terms, there were two forces for revenge working
in Dachuan. On the one hand, there were numerous people who
had been victimized by earlier political campaigns and government policies. Since the village's former Party secretary had
been the chief and most active implementor of these campaigns
and policies, he was held accountable by the survivors of political victimization. After the village was decollectivized, some of
these survivors began to amass considerable communal influence and even political clout beyond the village level. On the
other hand, community-wide frustration had been building up
over the decline in the village's historical status and its more
recent failure to obtain resettlement compensation. These
widely shared frustrations were manipulated by power contenders with personal grievances to vent. In the end, the accu-
mulated energy of personal grievances and collective frustrations was unleashed against an ultimate symbol of the Maoist
era and a familiar person who was perhaps all too easy to blame
for the village's troubled past.

The National Politics of Remembrance

   To relate the Dachuan material to the politics of remembrance at the national level, we must bear in mind that radical
socialism in Mao's China was marked by national chaos and personal tragedy. The Great Leap Forward from 1958 to 1961 precipitated famine on a gigantic scale, claiming 20–30 million lives
(Spence 1990: 583). The Cultural Revolution from 1966 to 1976
victimized at least one million people, many of whom did not
survive (Fairbank 1992: 402). Although two decades have passed
since Mao's death, honest and forthright accounts of these and
other traumas of the Maoist era are still strictly prohibited by
the Chinese party-state. At the local level, memories of past suffering are often repressed lest they open old wounds and threaten
the existing order of social relations.

   Despite these conditions of China's political culture, dangerous memories resist concealment. Arthur Kleinman, for example, has studied illness narratives as a medium of memorial articulation (1986, 1991, 1994). In examining accounts of personal history provided by Chinese patients, he finds that some narrators frequently associated physical pain and psychosomatic complaints with the terror and injustice they suffered during the Cultural Revolution. Conceptualizing the dynamic interaction of body and memory as "embodied memory" (1994), Kleinman regards the narration of political misfortunes through the body as a highly emotional form of moral protest against not only the original cause of pain but the mechanisms that perpetuate past injuries into the present.

Taking a different approach, Rubie Watson (1994: 65–86) has examined the composing of "secret history" in relation to the hardship of mourning personal or family anguish when it is caused by political persecution. Relating the impact of what she describes as "delayed mourning" to the seemingly spontaneous demonstrations on occasions marking the death of such official figures as Zhou Enlai and Hu Yaobang, her study suggests a strong correlation between open resistance on these public occasions of mourning and less dramatic, even secretive, forms of remembering individual suffering.

We have been reminded by other scholars (see, especially, Unger 1993; Ci 1994) that the Chinese Communist party-state is a shrewd and often relentless manipulator of society's memory. As the scholar Ci Jiwei has forcefully put it: "Memory is the internalization of history. History is the institution for the social regulation of memory. Those who control the means of regulating collective memory direct the course of future history. Not surprisingly, one of the biggest psycho-political projects undertaken by the Communist Party has been the restructuring of the Chinese memory through rewriting of Chinese history" (quoted by Schwarcz 1994: 50). To single out one of these "psycho-political projects" in relation to the Kong experience of reservoir resettlement, I draw attention to a government-sponsored drive to compile "local gazetteers" (di fang zhi).

What are local gazetteers? In origin, they derive from the practice, which became widespread in the third century A.D., of compiling biographies of local worthies along with their writings. At the same time, they derive from the practice of compiling basic information on local geography, population, customs, and revenue for submission to the central government. From about the tenth century onward, gazetteers became a vehicle for local elites and government officials to present their views on history and nearly every crucial aspect of life within the county, prefectural, and provincial units under a highly centralized bureaucratic system.

The tradition of compiling local gazetteers was discontinued in the People's Republic until the mid-1980's, when every province, prefecture, and county was urged by the central government to join a nationwide project to produce what are known as "new local gazetteers" (*xin fang zhi*). In 1992, a new gazetteer was completed in Yongjing county by a team of 24 local historians and archivists under the supervision of the county's magistrate and the head of its Party committee. Although this gazetteer has sixteen chapters, running over 1,000 pages, the countywide manhunt of 1958 and the devastating famine from 1959 to 1961 receive sketchy treatment. The misery-fraught resettlement during the construction of hydroelectric stations from 1958 to 1975 is trivialized by the absence of any detailed descriptions or critical afterthoughts. In other words, Yongjing's gazetteer compilers strictly adhered to the stipulations from above that in writing new local gazetteers the history of socialism under Mao must be treated with great caution and that the past achievements of the Communist Party must be emphasized (see, e.g., Lu Tianhong 1988; Ouyang Fa & Ding Jian 1986; Zhang Zhongying 1989). These stipulations were obviously intended to suppress mention of the terrible mistakes of Maoism and the cruelty of state-organized class struggles over a quarter of a century.

While the suffering of Yongjing's resettlers was ignored in the locally compiled public record, the political significance and macroeconomic benefits of the central government's three hydroelectric projects in Yongjing were glorified by mass media at the national and provincial levels, especially in a textbook used in primary schools throughout China and in a documentary film shown on a television channel serving the entire province of Gansu (see Chapter 4). The way Yongjing's history of reservoir resettlement has been manipulated in official representations at the county, provincial, and national levels indicates that the human cost of hydroelectric development in China as a whole is too high to be reasonably justified.

From the late 1950's to the late 1980's, ten million Chinese were displaced by the construction of major dams, reservoirs, and hydrostations.[1] Mostly rural residents, they were resettled against their will and severely affected by the loss of farmland. In 1989, seven million of these people were living below the official poverty line.[2] In the early 1990's, their impoverishment persisted under the double burden of inadequate compensation for their losses and resettlement on less productive land.[3] Exacerbating their plight has been a state policy of systematically suppressing mention of the human cost of hydropower development in the news media, documentary films, school textbooks, and academic research.

But official suppression of society's memory is not always effective. The transmission of memory involves a large armamentarium of symbolic resources and moral evaluations, in which the worth of political control itself can be questioned and even challenged. This is why I regard the new Confucius temple in Dachuan as a culturally inscribed monument to the suffering endured of the Kongs and, at the same time, as a religious milestone in their recovery from a deeply troubled past.

The Sacred Landmarks of Remembrance

In her book *The Art of Memory* (1966), Frances Yates has shown us how closely Western ideas of history and religion were once tied to memorable places, which were infused with mnemonic images such as a distinctive architecture structure and religious icons. First invented by Greco-Roman rhetoricians and then rediscovered by the Christian clergy of medieval Europe, this art of memory relied on a conscious manipulation of space to assist the tellers of mythical tales and religious stories to recall associated information as they spoke. Through mnemonic images that could be "beautiful or hideous" (Yates 1966: 10), notions of the past were deposited at and reinforced by memorable places. And by means of imagination, it was hoped that memories cultivated in this way would be readily recalled even in the absence of their architectural repositories (see also Fentress & Wickham 1992). A living example of this invented and subsequently reinvented art of memory can be found in the paintings, statues, and ritual objects of major Catholic churches. Such religious memorabilia may not be physically present when a believer travels to a foreign country, but their images and meaning stay in his or her mind.

The transmission of memory through architectural design, religious sites, familiar landmarks, and historical monuments is pivotal to the meaning of history in non-Western societies as well (see, e.g., Appadurai 1981: 201–19; Harwood 1976: 783–96; Vansina 1985). For example, a study by Gillian Feeley-Harnik (1991: 121–40) has established the connection of toponymy, royal tombs, and genealogical claims to the workings of social hierarchy in Madagascar. Roger Bastide (1978) has traced the vestiges of African culture among urban blacks in Brazil and Haiti to a spatial dimension of communal memory—shrines, images of deities, and dance halls. Renato Rosaldo, in his book (1980) based on fieldwork in the Philippines, shows that notions of the past among a mountain people are "meticulously mapped onto the landscape," to the extent that their narratives of flight from and attacks on Japanese troops in 1945 constitute mental excursions back to "every rock, hill, and stream where they ate, rested, or slept" (1981: 48).

In China, memories of historical times merge with memories of sacred landmarks in an intimate way. In point of fact, the fate of religious sites is a constant theme in Chinese literature, drama, oral folklore, and historical writings. Recurring descriptions of the ruin or splendor of royal temples, pilgrimage sites, and community shrines suggest a powerful analogy to the shifting fortunes of state, society, and families (Chang 1983; DeBernardi 1992; Faure 1987; Ryckmans 1986; Tuan 1977). This analogy is aptly embodied by Dachuan's Confucius temple, whose fate in a recent past was deeply entwined with China's experiment with radical socialism.

It should be made clear here that the destruction of temples occurred frequently enough in Chinese history that it cannot be considered a phenomenon unique to the Maoist regime. Underpinning the cycles of temple construction, destruction, and reconstruction prior to the mid-twentieth century were the shifting attitudes of state authorities and Chinese scholars toward various religious traditions and their institutions (De Groot 1892–1910; Duara 1991: 67–83; Feuchtwang 1992; Jordan & Overmyer 1986; Welch 1965; Weller 1987; C. K. Yang 1961). However, a key difference between earlier iconoclasts and Maoist revolutionaries is that the former took a selective approach to religion while the latter espoused an indiscriminately antireligious policy. The numerous Maoist antireligious campaigns were aimed at achieving a clean slate, a total break with traditional ways and ideologies represented by Taoism, Buddhism, local cults, the state cult of Confucianism, and Christianity introduced by Westerners.

The recently reinstated worship of Confucius in the Dachuan area is not an isolated case of religious renewal in a rather remote part of China. After three decades of state-organized suppression, Taoism, Buddhism, Islam, and Christianity are now alive and well in the People's Republic. The resurgence of popular religion in particular tells a dramatic story of cultural rejuvenation. With the reinstallment of religious icons at local temples that are devoted to the worship of medicine gods, fertility goddesses, flood-control deities, and many other supernatural beings, popular religion has reestablished a stronghold in Chinese villages and market towns.

Helen Siu (1989b: 195–212) has written that during her 1986 fieldwork, she was struck by the "aggressive public display" of religious rituals and festivals in a market town of the Pearl River delta. She stresses that not only ordinary people but local officials participated in these rituals (see also Siu 1990: 765–94). At the village level, Stevan Harrell (1988: 8–14) has informed us that popular religion in a rural community he visited in southern Sichuan province had become, by 1988, "a normal, matter-of-fact part of people's life" (quoted by MacInnis 1989: 373). He estimates that 80 percent of the local households had installed traditional altars, "dedicated to Heaven and Country, the Stove God, the Ancestors of the Lineage, and the Lord of Earth" (*ibid.*). And in a vivid description of her research in the rural areas around the city of Wenzhou from 1991 to 1993, Mayfair Yang (1993) observes that the rapid economic development in these areas is paralleled by an equally rapid revival of Taoist and Buddhist temples, coupled with the return of shrines devoted to various gods and goddesses, the renewal of lineage organizations, and the jubilant ritual celebration of festivals in the lunar calendar. In Wenzhou, she argues, "economic privatism has paradoxically produced, not so much individualism, as a great deal of community participation in the rebuilding of local infrastructure and traditional culture" (1993: 2).

The rapid proliferation of popular religion has obviously alarmed the Chinese party-state. One of its responses has been to issue vehement denunciations, through news media and anti-superstition literature, of the construction of elaborate tombs and village shrines,[4] the reinstated worship of rain gods,[5] and the circulation of apocalyptic prophecies.[6] An official anti-superstition handbook stated accusingly in 1991 that the practices of geomancy, fortune-telling, and shamanistic healing were rapidly resumed in the 1980's by older practitioners with a growing horde of young apprentices.[7] This problem was attributed to local officials who "open one eye and close the other" in dealing with manifestations of "feudal superstition." The handbook took particular exception to the conversion of many young

Chinese to "feudal superstition." It cited the case of Pingguo county in Guangxi province, which had a total of 21,000 "female shamans" (wu po) and "magical men" (shen han) in 1989, about 60 percent of whom were of a relatively young age.

There is little doubt that the Chinese social landscape has taken on an intensified religious atmosphere. But it would be too hasty to conclude that popular religion has been miraculously restored to its pre-Communist state. With the deaths of an older generation familiar with traditional ritual knowledge and the destruction of religious texts and artifacts during the Cultural Revolution, the organization of temple cults and religious festivals does not always proceed easily. Furthermore, no matter what terms, concepts, or theories we employ for understanding the return of popular religion to the public sphere of Chinese life, we must not overlook the elements of cultural invention attached to it.

Cultural invention is certainly a vital component in the social organization of the Kongs in the Dachuan area, as well as in their religious response to sociopolitical changes. Such inventiveness is apparent when we consider their efforts to expand the cult of Confucius by deciding on an unconventional arrangement of spirit tablets and by creating a double liturgy to change a lineage-focused ceremony into a public festival. Through cultural innovations like these, the Kong lineage established, at a fixed spot and time, one of the largest religious festivities in the living memory of the villagers residing in the valley of Yongjing county.

In organizing the widely publicized and enthusiastically attended celebration of Confucius's birthday, the leaders of the Dachuan-based cult of the ancient sage also turned their enterprise into one of Yongjing's largest religious associations, whose institutional bases, ritual services, and fund-raising networks had been revived since the mid-1980's at five locally renowned and refurbished temples.[8] By becoming active agents in the sphere of popular religion, these Kong leaders have extended their lineage's influence and networks of connections into a vital domain of rural life. Broadly speaking, this religious domain of village life is becoming a strong, alternative base of power and authority precisely because it is tied to the increasingly noticeable assertion of local identity, voluntary associations, and community autonomy in the world's last major Communist country.

Notes

Chapter One

1. This dam project, known as the Yanguoxia Hydroelectric Station, was undertaken around the same time that another large dam was being constructed at the Sanmenxia, in downstream Henan province. These were the first hydroelectric and multipurpose dams ever built on the Yellow River (see Greer 1979; Wang Weimin 1989).

2. In 1945, a joint Sino-American team of hydraulic engineers was sent by the Nationalist government to survey various sites, including a spot not far from Dachuan, as part of a plan to build modern dams along the Yellow River. This plan became impractical with the outbreak of all-out civil war in 1946 between the Nationalists and the Communists (see Yongjing County Gazetteer Committee, 1992: 16, 8).

3. Caused by the Great Leap Forward (1958–61), a devastating famine raged throughout China, claiming 20–30 million lives (see Kane 1988).

4. See Chapter 3 for a discussion of Mao Zedong's reasons for launching this political campaign.

5. The Kongs in other parts of China were identified in the 1937 edition of the Kong clan genealogy as belonging to ten main branches (pai), all named after the places where they initially settled after leaving Qufu (e.g., Guangdong/Branch, ling nan pai. Many smaller segments were attached to the ten main branches, partly owing to further migration and resettlement. These smaller segments were scattered in nearly every Chinese province (see Kong Decheng 1937).

6. Dachuan was undoubtedly an economically backward village in 1992. But some local residents, especially village cadres, had prospered. For instance, the heads of the village's ten most well-to-do households in 1992 included the local Party boss, three former village cadres, two retired bureaucrats from county government agencies, and three private entrepreneurs whose sons were working as officials beyond the village level. For the impact of economic reforms on the administrative power of village cadres and on the disparity of personal wealth in rural China see Huang (1989), Yan (1992), Kelliher (1992), Chan, Madsen, & Unger (1992), and Ruf (1994).

7. Important excerpts from Halbwachs's first two memory studies have been brilliantly translated by Lewis Coser and published under the title *On Collective Memory* (1992). An English translation of his entire third study of memory was published in 1980 under the title *The Collective Memory*, with an insightful introduction by Mary Douglas.

Chapter Two

1. This Kong-Muslim community is called *xin si*, or "New Mosque" village, a nearly uninhabitable place surrounded by high, barren mountains.

2. On two occasions, the Kong Huihui tried to return to Dachuan. In 1948 they tried to reclaim property, to renovate their ancestral graveyard, and to resettle in Dachuan. The Han Kongs flatly refused to allow this and a lawsuit followed, which the Kong Huihui lost. Then in 1956 they tried again to return to Dachuan, apparently thinking that the collective farming system (still at the "high-level cooperatives" stage) might be more accommodating. To avoid trouble, the township government turned down their request. Over the years, only one Kong Huihui household was allowed to return to Dachuan, when, in the late 1970's, its male head was appointed by the county government to a senior position in the people's commune under whose jurisdiction Dachuan's collectives operated.

3. The 1930's appears to have been a time when many enormous genealogies involving people from much of the country were being compiled (see Eberhard 1962).

Chapter Three

1. The major cause of these frequent appointments to the "chief of security" (*bao zhang*) position was the constant conscription by several

military factions in Gansu. One of the duties required of but hardly achievable by the chief of security was to raise funds to compensate families of men who were drafted.

2. According to a population survey I consulted in Yongjing's archives, the county had 110,062 people in 1953. The four Kong settlements, each within easy reach of the county seat, contained more than 5,000 Kongs.

3. In 1992, the Kongs of Dachuan sent three letters to Kong Decheng asking him to inscribe this central board, but when I interviewed Kong Decheng in August 1993, he said that he had never received the letters. I suspect that these letters were intercepted by the postal service in China. Kong Decheng is known to be a staunch supporter of the Nationalist government. Until early 1993, he headed Taiwan's Examination Yuan. When asked whether, now that he had retired, he would return to Qufu to revisit his hometown, he replied sadly that whatever he wanted to see could be found in his memory but not in Qufu. His unwillingness to return to Qufu may be attributable to the many distressing events that had occurred there during the Cultural Revolution. One of them was the destruction of the Kong clan cemetery. On November 29, 1966, Red Guards from the Qufu area and radical students from Beijing converged on the cemetery to drag Confucius's remains from his tomb. It took them two days to open the gigantic tomb, only to find nothing inside it. But at the tomb of Kong Lingyi, Kong Decheng's father, the grave robbers retrieved three well-preserved bodies: Kong Lingyi, his wife, and his concubine, the last being Kong Decheng's biological mother. These bodies were burned on the spot. The discovery of gold, jade, and other valuables in the cemetery resulted in four months of looting and the destruction of 4,000 Kong tombs (see Ya Zi & Liang Zi 1992: 181–289).

4. In an illustrated collection of brief biographies of Confucius's personal disciples, its authors (Zhang & Jin 1991) point out that, except for their name and birthplace, 30 of the 72 disciples cannot be further described because of the absence of textual data.

5. For the historical transformation and orthodox arrangement of spirit tablets in government-run Confucius temples, see Shryock (1966) and Wilson (1995a).

Chapter Four

1. The loss of farmland was compensated according to a valuation based on the estimated potential harvest within three years.

2. The records left by this resettlement committee are kept by two

local archive bureaus, one under the Linxia Prefectural Government and the other in Yongjing county.

3. Judging by place-names kept in a genealogical record and sketches drawn by local informants, the tombs of these local founding ancestors were built at separate grounds, which indicates the beginning of the Kong lineage's segmentation into four main branches. In addition, the tombs of later generations at these burial grounds were built in neat rows to distinguish the generational ranks of the dead. In a study of north China lineages, Myron Cohen (1990: 509–34) discusses an identical tomb arrangement, explaining that the typical burial ground in a village he studied had a triangular shape, with the tomb of a branch's focal ancestor occupying the apex and the tombs of later generations descending from that of the focal ancestor.

4. I am informed by Myron Cohen that the practice of entombing a stick, brick, or stone with the inscribed name of the dead on it was once rather common in north China. The inscribed object was used in creating a second grave for an ancestor whose remains had been buried in a lineage's original graveyard but whose symbolic presence was needed by a segment of the lineage to establish its own graveyard (see Cohen 1990: 513). However, the Kong case is different in two ways. First, the inscribed sticks were used in place of ancestral remains that could not be rescued at the time of resettlement. Second, a tomb containing an inscribed stick does not constitute an ancestor's second grave but his only grave once his original tomb had been flooded.

Chapter Five

1. Personal or household-based compensation is unlikely to be granted in the near future because of its high cost. There are now over ten million people in mainland China who are identified by state agencies as "reservoir relocatees." The majority of them are deeply impoverished and need compensation to shake off poverty.

2. His uncle tried repeatedly to reclaim the family's property after he was released from prison and told that he had been wronged. County officials rejected his appeals, however, fearing that since there were many similar cases, approval could set off a series of property claims detrimental to the existing social order.

Chapter Six

1. The booklet is entitled *Rites of Offering Sacrifices to Our Holy Ancestor (Ji shengzu yishi)*.

2. The utterance of Chinese sounds can be also transcribed by *pin-yin*, the romanization system used in this book. *Pinyin* was officially endorsed by the People's Republic in 1958. Since 1979, the Chinese have largely succeeded in persuading Western publishers to adopt this system in place of previous systems, turning Mao Tse-tung into Mao Zedong. In mainland China, *pinyin* serves several practical purposes. It helps to specify pronunciations of written characters in dictionaries, it serves as a device for introducing children to reading, and it functions as a supplement to ordinary Chinese script in contexts such as slogans on posts, bus-stop and road signs, and place-names. It is shown beside or under characters for the benefit of semiliterate or dialect-speaking readers who can use this information to decipher characters with which they are unfamiliar, or to learn the standard pronunciation of words that have different pronunciations. The system is not intended to replace the logographic Chinese script.

3. The relationship described here between older ritualists and their younger assistants or other people attending this ritual ceremony is characteristic of other Chinese religious ceremonies. My description of this relationship is not intended to portray the Kong ceremony as unique, but to bring out the esoteric nature of ritual knowledge in a situated context.

4. In parts of mainland China, the traditional script has been staging a comeback. In coastal regions such as Fujian and Guangdong provinces, which have attracted large investments from Hong Kong and Taiwan (where the traditional script is used exclusively), billboards, tourist maps, commercial catalogues, and business cards are increasingly converted into "complex characters."

Chapter Seven

1. This hesitation relates in part to a controversy in anthropology over the question of whether genealogical terminology represents social categories of individuals in unilineal descent systems. See Roger Keesing (1975: 119) for a concise summary of this debate.

2. A bibliographical study by Taga Akigoro in 1960 lists nearly 3,000 genealogies, of which about 500 are in the libraries of mainland China, close to 1,000 in the United States, and more than 1,200 in Japan (quoted by Meskill 1970: 140). The sudden appearance of private genealogies in the public domain during the 1930's has been explained by Meskill in terms of wartime chaos (Meskill 1970: 139). However, Zhang Xiumin, a leading specialist in mainland China on the history of Chinese printing, attributes their appearance to the aggressive purchasing efforts of domestic book dealers to meet the orders, and make

handsome profits, from Japanese and American libraries (Zhang [1962] 1990: 200). By 1949, Zhang says, the number of genealogical records at Columbia University alone far surpassed the holdings of the National Library in Beijing, which then had 353 genealogies (ibid., 206). The National Library in Beijing now has about 2,250 genealogies, excluding duplicates (Liu Liming 1993: 156).

3. The autumn Equinox was interpreted in the same manner, but the spring sacrifices to the dead were of greater importance.

4. In a recent, well-researched work on Chinese family rituals, a passage in a fifteenth-century text is cited by Patricia Ebrey as saying that the commemoration of the birth anniversaries of the dead was a prevalent practice (Ebrey 1991: 175). However, it seems to me that this practice was primarily devoted to ancestors within a few generations rather than those who were many generations removed. The reason is that both birth and death anniversaries of distant ancestors were hard to determine, even assuming they were worthy of remembering at all. The exceptional cases were those extraordinarily famous ancestors whose life histories achieved recognition by official historians.

5. These "ancestor charts," which have staged a comeback in the Dachuan area, are known as *shen zhu*, an old Chinese term for spirit tablets. A typical chart of this kind is made of a room-sized cloth screen on which the names of dead ancestors and their wives are written in rectangular boxes. The chart, usually embellished with depictions of splendid palaces, broad streets, and pine trees, is taken to the courtyard and unfurled from roof to floor during the death ritual ceremony performed at the home of the dead before his or her corpse is transferred to the burial ground. Thus while this ritual occasion is intended to mourn the most recent death, the deceased is remembered together with forebears. The rectangular boxes are shaped exactly like spirit tablets and are separated in generational rows. On such charts, a vertical line is drawn across the name of a dead person with blood taken from the back of a descendant's neck. The local explanation is that the blood is drawn through the names on the ancestor charts to comfort the dead with a physical symbol of family continuity.

6. Similar ancestor charts were found by Myron Cohen during his 1986–87 research trips to a village of Hebei province. According to Cohen, these charts customarily were displayed in commemoration of ancestors for three days during the Chinese lunar New Year. All such charts, described by Cohen as "ancestral scrolls," were owned by individual families, not by lineages or other multifamily groups (1990: 515). In the village of Dachuan, the situation was sharply different. There, the Kong ancestor charts, eight altogether, were not displayed during

the Chinese lunar New Year but during funerary rituals. All ancestor charts in Dachuan belonged to multifamily groups, although each of them was kept at the home of an individual family whose head occupied the most senior generational rank within that multifamily unit. When a death occurred within that unit, the chart would be sent to and displayed at the home of the dead—which in some cases was outside Dachuan—for registering his or her name and for staging the ceremony to initiate the ritual transfer of the corpse. This happened in 1992, when a funerary ceremony was held in the city of Lanzhou for an old man who had moved with his wife and children out of Dachuan more than twenty years earlier.

7. Commenting on his experience in a village in Taiwan, Hugh Baker says that there appears to have been a belief that the ancestor might be present wherever his name was written down, and this would accord with the almost sacred quality the written word came to acquire in China. "When I asked permission to copy down the genealogy of the Sheung Shui Liao lineage, one old man said to me: 'I don't know if the ancestors will like it in London.' He clearly felt uneasy that the ancestors would be taken back with me in the copy" (H. Baker 1979: 83–84).

8. Four recent studies of Chinese genealogies kept by more than thirty large lineages in pre-1949 China show that extraordinary efforts were undertaken to keep genealogies secret (He Guangyue 1991; Liu Youping 1991; Luo & Nien 1991; Shen 1991). One extreme method was to destroy older genealogies when new ones were compiled (He Guangyue 1991: 108–9). The more usual methods involved carved seals, codified serial numbers, and secret storage places. Quite often, reliable keepers were appointed who could be severely punished if the records were damaged or fell into the hands of outsiders.

Chapter Eight

1. Some villagers also had seen statues of Mao in the county seat and Lanzhou. But these were icons of a personality cult, involving no prayers, prostration, or incense burning.

2. As indicated by its name, the opera originated in Shaanxi province, which is just east of Gansu. The language of the opera's songs and dialogues can be traced to the dialect of Xi'an, Shaanxi's capital. This form of opera dates back at least to the sixteenth century (see Mackerras 1990: 54–59).

3. Shaanxi opera is by far the most popular form of theater in Gansu and Ningxia. It spread from Shaanxi to northwest China, according to the Japanese scholar Tanaka Issei (1981, 1985), through commerce, es-

pecially the sponsorship of performances by local and traveling businessmen during temple festivities as a marketing strategy to attract customers.

Chapter Nine

1. This figure has been cited by Tian & Lin (1986: 185) and by Zhang Yue (1988: 40).

2. The Leading Group of Economic Development in Poor Areas (LGEDPA), a poverty-relief agency operating under China's State Council, set, in 1989, the absolute poverty line at a range from 150 to 350 yuan in annual per capita income, depending on the varying costs in different regions for basic necessities such as food, clothing, and shelter. Using the statistics provided by LGEDPA, the World Bank (1992) estimated that between 86 and 103 million people, roughly 9 percent of China's population, lived in absolute poverty during 1985–90.

3. Personal communications with researchers working for the Chinese Ministry of Agriculture and State Council during the "Food, Consumption, and Social Change in Chinese Society" workshop at the Fairbank Center for East Asian Research, Harvard University, August 8–19, 1994.

4. In a *China Peasant News* (*Zhongguo nongmin bao*) article (May 3, 1989, p. 4), Wang Bing criticizes the increase in elaborate tombs and new temples in rural China. He says that the brand-new temples, all installed with elaborately molded clay statues, have become typical specks on the landscape in more than 1,000 villages surrounding the city of Wenzhou in the coastal province of Zhejiang. On the issue of expansive tombs, see Li Shengxian's article "Farewell to the Chair-Shaped Tombs" (*Tianjin Daily*, Aug. 26, 1990, p. 6), and Yang Weimin's article "Thousands of Tombs Appeared at Baiyunshan" (*People's Daily*, Aug. 27, 1989, p. 8).

5. See Yun Cai's article "Remember to Get Rid of Ignorance Together with Poverty" (*Chinese Culture Newspaper, Zhongguo wenhua bao*, Mar. 16, 1988, p. 2), and He Chi's article "Smashing Feudal Superstition and Promoting Agricultural Science" (*Gansu Daily*, Feb. 11, 1992, p. 4.

6. One prophecy is given a rather detailed description in an official anti-superstition handbook (Tianjin Municipal Party Committee 1991). It is said in this handbook that urban residents in several cities of northeast China were misled into panic buying by a widespread rumor from April to May 1988 that a white snake had appeared on major highways in the form of a beautiful young woman to inform drivers that a

year of great disasters was imminent. One of the many consequences of this widely circulated prophecy was the sellout of canned peaches because in Chinese the word for peaches (*tao*) and the word for escape are phonetically identical. In other words, buying peaches was a way to seek deliverance from the impending disasters. Another widely cited case of prophecy involved thousands of patients who, in 1989, flocked to and prayed at a small pond in Sheyang county, Jiangsu province, where the unusually loud noise of mating frogs was proclaimed to be a sign of the approaching advent of the seven immortals from heaven on a healing mission.

7. Tianjin Municipal Party Committee (1991).

8. These temples include: (1) two prayer halls rebuilt in Liujiaxia village by the Society of Virtues (*gong de lin*), a self-organized multicommunity association whose 530 regular members are known as *ju shi*, "home-staying" Buddhists; (2) the White Pagoda Monastery (*bai ta si*), whose three halls and a white pagoda were rebuilt by four villages and then turned over to twelve ordained Han Chinese priests practicing Tibetan Buddhism; (3) three halls at the Evergreen Temple (*chang qing guan*), the refurbishment of which was initiated by five self-proclaimed Taoists and supported by about ten villages; (4) the Temple of Lady Jinhua (*jing hua miao*), whose three halls were rebuilt by 24 villages; and, (5) seven large-scale halls at the Luojia Cave (*luo jia dong*), rebuilt by two villages with financial and material contributions from more than twenty nearby villages and a market town. At least one large festival was held annually at each of these temple sites. It should be added that the largest religious site in Yongjing is a Buddhist cave-temple complex called Binglingsi. Unlike the five temple sites listed above that were rebuilt and managed by local people, Binglingsi was managed, as late as 1995, by a government agency that provided the monks in residence with a monthly allowance. Yongjing also had, in 1992, 63 mosques in predominantly Hui communities. The Hui constituted 12 percent of Yongjing's population.

References

Ackerman, William, ed. 1973. *Man-Made Lakes: Their Problems and Environmental Effects.* Washington, D.C.: American Geophysical Union.

Ahern, Emily. 1975. "The Power and Pollution of Chinese Women." In *Women in Chinese Society.* Ed. Margery Wolf & Roxane Witke. Stanford, Calif.: Stanford University Press.

Anagnost, Ann. 1987. "Politics and Magic in Contemporary China." *Modern China*, 11(2): 147–76.

Appadurai, Arjun. 1981. "The Past as a Sacred Resource." *Man*, n.s., 16 (June): 201–19.

Aron, Raymond. 1970. *Main Currents in Sociological Thought.* New York: Doubleday.

Baker, Hugh D. R. 1977. "Extended Kinship in the Traditional City." In *The City in Late Imperial China.* Ed. G. William Skinner. Stanford, Calif.: Stanford University Press.

————. 1979. *Chinese Kinship and Family.* London: Macmillan.

Baker, Keith M. 1990. *Inventing the French Revolution.* Cambridge, Eng.: Cambridge University Press.

Bartlett, Frederic. [1932] 1954. *Remembering: A Study in Experimental and Social Psychology.* Cambridge, Eng.: Cambridge University Press.

Bastide, Roger. 1978. *The African Religions of Brazil: Toward a Sociology of the Interpretation of Civilizations.* Baltimore: Johns Hopkins University Press.

Bodnar, John. 1989. "Power and Memory in Oral History: Workers and Managers at Studebaker." *Journal of American History*, 75(4): 1201–21.

Bol, Peter K. 1992. *This Culture of Ours: Intellectual Transition in T'ang and Sung China*. Stanford, Calif.: Stanford University Press.

Brown, Roger, & James Kulik. 1982. "Flashbulb Memory." In *Memory Observed: Remembering in Natural Context*. Ed. Ulric Neisser. San Francisco: W. H. Freeman.

Burke, Peter. 1989. "History as Social Memory." In *Memory: History, Culture, and the Mind*. Ed. Thomas Butler. Oxford, Eng.: Basil Blackwell.

Chaffee, John. 1985. *The Thorny Gate of Learning in Sung China*. Cambridge, Mass.: Harvard University Press.

Chan, Anita, Richard Madsen, & Jonathan Unger. 1984. *Chen Village: The Recent History of a Peasant Community in Mao's China*. Berkeley: University of California Press.

———. 1992. *Chen Village: Under Mao and Deng*. Berkeley: University of California Press.

Chang, K. C. 1983. *Art, Myth, and Ritual: The Path to Political Authority in Ancient China*. Cambridge, Mass.: Harvard University Press.

Chao, Yuen-ren. 1968. *Language and Symbols*. Cambridge, Eng.: Cambridge University Press.

Cheng, Chin-chuan. 1977. "In Defense of Teaching Simplified Characters." *Journal of Chinese Linguistics*, 5: 314–54.

Chesneaux, Jean. 1971. *Secret Societies in China*. London: Heinemann.

China Handbook Editorial Board. 1950. *China Yearbook*. New York: Rockport Press.

Chuang, Ying-chang. 1990. "A Comparison of Hokkien and Hakka Ancestor Worship." *Bulletin of the Institute of Ethnology* (Academia Sinica), 69: 130–60.

Ci Jiwei. 1994. *Dialectics of the Chinese Revolution: From Utopianism to Hedonism*. Stanford, Calif.: Stanford University Press.

Cohen, Gillian. 1989. *Memory in the Real World*. London: Erlbaum.

Cohen, Myron L. 1990. "Lineage Organization in North China." *Journal of Asian Studies*, 49(3): 509–34.

Connerton, Paul. 1989. *How Societies Remember*. Cambridge, Eng.: Cambridge University Press.

Coser, Lewis. 1992. "Introduction: Maurice Halbwachs, 1877–1945." In M. Halbwachs, *On Collective Memory*. Chicago: University of Chicago Press.

Creel, Herrlee G. 1949. *Confucius: The Man and the Myth*. New York: John Day.

Crook, Isabel, & David Cook. 1959. *Revolution in a Chinese Village: Ten Mile Inn*. London: Routledge.

———. 1979. *Ten Mile Inn: Mass Movement in a Chinese Village*. New York: Pantheon.

de Bary, Wm. T. 1959. "Some Common Tendencies in Neo-Confucianism." In *Confucianism in Action*. Ed. David S. Nivison & Arthur F. Wright. Stanford, Calif.: Stanford University Press.

De Groot, J. J. M. 1892–1910. *The Religious Systems of China* (6 vols.). Leyden: Brill.

DeBernardi, Jean. 1992. "Space and Time in Chinese Religious Culture." *History of Religions*, 31(3): 247–68.

DeFrancis, John. 1977. "Language and Script Reform." In *Advances in the Creation and Revision of Writing Systems*. Ed. Joshua Fishman. New York: Mouton.

Deng, Zihui. 1955. *Report on the Multiple-Purpose Plan for Permanently Controlling the Yellow River and Exploring Its Water Resources*. Beijing: Foreign Languages Press.

Diamond, Norma. 1969. *K'un Shen: A Taiwan Village*. New York: Holt, Rinehart.

———. 1988. "The Miao and Poison: Interactions on China's Frontier." *Ethnology*, 27(1): 1–25.

Dirlik, Arif. 1978. *Revolution and History: Origins of Marxist Historiography in China, 1919–1937*. Berkeley: University of California Press.

Dong Junlun & Jiang Yuan. 1992. *Kongzi shi jia* (The Confucius Clan). Beijing: Zuojia Press.

Douglas, Mary. 1980. "Introduction: Maurice Halbwachs (1877–1945)." In M. Halbwachs, *The Collective Memory*. Trans. & ed. Francis J. Ditter, Jr., & Vida Yadzi Ditter. New York: Harper & Row.

Duara, Prasenjit. 1991. "Knowledge and Power in the Discourse of Modernity: The Campaigns Against Popular Religion in Early Twentieth-Century China." *Journal of Asian Studies*, 50(1): 67–83.

Durkheim, Emile. [1911] 1954. *The Elementary Forms of the Religious Life*. London: Allen & Unwin.

———. [1930] 1964. *The Division of Labor in Society*. New York: Free Press.

Ebbinghaus, Hermann. [1885] 1964. *Memory: A Contribution to Experimental Psychology*. New York: Dover.

Eberhard, Wolfram. 1962. *Social Mobility in Traditional China*. Leyden: Brill.

Ebrey, Patricia. 1986. "The Early Stages of Descent Group Organization." In *Kinship Organization in Late Imperial China 1000–1940*.

Ed. Patricia Ebrey & James L. Watson. Berkeley: University of California Press.

————. 1991a. *Confucianism and Family Rituals in Imperial China.* Princeton, N.J.: Princeton University Press.

————. 1991b. *Chu Hsi' Family Rituals.* Princeton, N.J.: Princeton University Press.

Ekvall, Robert. 1938. *Gateway to Tibet.* Harrisburg, Penn.: Christian Publications.

Elvin, Mark. 1991. "The Inner World of 1830." *Daedalus.* 120(1): 33–61. Reprinted in Tu Wei-ming, ed., *The Living Tree: The Changing Meaning of Being Chinese Today.* Stanford, Calif.: Stanford University Press [1994].

Fairbank, John K. 1983. *The United States and China.* Cambridge, Mass.: Harvard University Press.

————. 1992.*China: A New History.* Cambridge, Mass.: Harvard University Press.

Fan Wei, ed. 1990. *Qufu: The Native Place of Confucius.* Beijing: Cultural Relics Press (in English and Chinese).

Farmer, Paul. 1992. *AIDS and Accusation: Haiti and the Geography of Blame.* Berkeley: University of California Press.

Faure, Bernard. 1987. "Space and Place in Chinese Religious Traditions." *History of Religions,* 26(4): 337–56.

Feeley-Harnik, Gillian. 1991. "Finding Memories in Madagascar." In *Images of Memory: On Remembering and Representation.* Ed. Susanne Kuchler & Walter Melion. Washington, D.C.: Smithsonian Institution Press.

Fentress, James, & Chris Wickham. 1992. *Social Memory.* Oxford, Eng.: Blackwell.

Feuchtwang, Stephan. 1974. *An Anthropological Analysis of Chinese Geomancy.* Vientiane: Vithagna.

————. 1977. "School-Temple, and City God." In *The City in Late Imperial China.* Ed. G. William Skinner. Stanford, Calif.: Stanford University Press.

————. 1992. *The Imperial Metaphor: Popular Religion in China.* London: Routledge.

Feuerwerker, Albert. 1968. "China's History in Marxian Dress." In *History in Communist China.* Ed. Albert Feuerwerker. Cambridge, Mass.: MIT Press.

Fields, Lanny. 1978. *Tso Tsung-T'ang and the Muslims: Statecraft in Northwest China, 1868–1880.* Kingston, Ont.: Limestone Press.

Firth, Raymond. 1967. *Tikopia Ritual and Belief.* London: Allen & Unwin.

Fortune, Reo. 1963. *Sorcerers of Dobu*. New York: Dutton.

Freedman, Maurice. 1958. *Lineage Organization in Southeastern China*. London: Athlone.

———. 1966. *Chinese Lineage and Society: Fukien and Kwangtung*. London: Athlone.

Friedman, Edward, Paul G. Pickowicz, & Mark Selden, with Kay Ann Johnson. 1991. *Chinese Village, Socialist State*. New Haven, Conn.: Yale University Press.

Fung, Yu-lan. 1952. *A History of Chinese Philosophy* (2 vols.). Trans. Derk Bodde. Princeton, N.J.: Princeton University Press.

Fustel de Coulanges, N. D. [1864] 1956. *The Ancient City: A Study on the Religion, Laws, and Institutions of Greece and Rome*. New York: Doubleday.

Gansu Economic Planning Commission. 1987. "On Planned Solutions to the Existing Problems of Resettlement Caused by the Liujia Gorge, Yanguo Gorge, and Bapan Gorge Reservoirs" (in Chinese).

Gansu Hydraulic Society. 1988. "An Assessment of Planned Solutions to the Existing Problems of Resettlement Caused by the Liujia Gorge, Yanguo Gorge, and Bapan Gorge Reservoirs" (in Chinese).

Gardner, Howard. 1989. *To Open Minds: Chinese Clues to the Dilemma of Contemporary Education*. New York: Basic Books.

Geertz, Clifford. 1957. "Ethos, World-View and the Analysis of Sacred Symbols." *Antioch Review*, 17: 421–37.

George, Kenneth. 1990. "Felling a Tree with a New Ax: Writing and the Reshaping of Ritual Song Performance in Upland Sulawesi." *Journal of American Folklore*, 103(407): 2–23.

Gladney, Dru. 1991. *Muslim Chinese: Ethnic Nationalism in the People's Republic*. Cambridge, Mass.: Harvard University Press.

Goldman, Merle. 1967. *Literary Dissent in Communist China*. Cambridge, Mass.: Harvard University Press.

Goldman, Merle, Timothy Cheek, & Carol Mamrin, eds. 1983. *China's Intellectuals and the State: In Search of a New Relationship*. Cambridge, Mass.: Harvard University.

Goody, Jack (with Ian Watt). 1968. "The Consequences of Literacy." In *Literacy in Traditional Societies*. Ed. Jack Goody. Cambridge, Eng.: Cambridge University Press.

———. 1977. *The Domestication of the Savage Mind*. Cambridge, Eng.: Cambridge University Press.

———. 1986. *The Logic of Writing and the Organization of Society*. Cambridge, Eng.: Cambridge University Press.

———. 1987. *The Interface Between the Written and the Oral*. Cambridge, Eng.: Cambridge University Press.

Greenhalgh, Susan. 1993. "The Peasantization of the One-Child Policy in Shaanxi." In *Chinese Families in the Post-Mao Era*. Ed. Deborah Davis & Stevan Harrell. Berkeley: University of California Press.

Greer, Charles. 1979. *Water Management in the Yellow River Basin of China*. Austin: University of Texas Press.

Halbwachs, Maurice. [1925] 1952. *Les Cadres sociaux de la mémoire*. Paris: Presses Universitaires de France.

————. 1941. *La Topographie légendaire des Évangiles en Terre Sainte: etude de mémoire collective*. Paris: Presses Universitaires de France.

————. [1950] 1980. *The Collective Memory*. Trans. & ed. Francis J. Ditter, Jr., & Vida Yadzdi Ditter. New York: Harper & Row.

————. 1992. *On Collective Memory*. Trans. Lewis Coser. Chicago: University of Chicago Press.

Handler, Richard, & Jocelyn Linnekin. 1984. "Traditions, Genuine or Spurious." *Journal of American Folklore*, 97: 273–90.

Hanson, Allan. 1989. "The Making of the Maori: Cultural Invention and Its Logic." *American Anthropologist*, 91(4): 890–902.

Hardwood, Frances. 1976. "Myth, Memory, and the Oral Tradition: Cicero in the Trobriands," *American Anthropologist*, 78(4): 783–96.

Harrell, Stevan. 1987. "On the Holes in Chinese Genealogies." *Late Imperial China*, 8(2): 53.

————. 1988. "Joint Ethnographic Fieldwork in Southern Sichuan." *China Exchange News*, 16(3): 8–14.

Hartford, Kathleen. 1985. "Socialist Agriculture is Dead; Long Live Socialist Agriculture! Organizational Transformations in Rural China." In *The Political Economy of Reform in Post-Mao China*. Ed. Elizabeth J. Perry & Christine Wong. Cambridge, Mass.: Harvard University Press.

He Chi. 1992. "Smash Feudal Superstitions and Promote Science for Agricultural Development" (Puochu minxin tichang keji xin nong). *Gansu Daily (Gansu ribao)*. Feb. 11, p. 4.

He Guangyue, ed. 1991. *Encyclopedia of Chinese Names: The Surname Chen (Zhongguo xingshi tongshu: chen xing)*. Changsha: Sanhuan Press.

He Lingxiu, ed. 1981. *The Archetype of Feudal Landlords: A Study of the Kong Mansion (Fengjian guizu dadizhu de dianxing)*. Beijing: Chinese Academy of Social Sciences Press.

Herzfeld, Michael. 1985. *The Poetics of Manhood*. Princeton, N.J.: Princeton University Press.

————. 1986. *Ours Once More: Folklore, Ideology, and the Making of Modern Greece*. New York: Pella.

Hill, Jonathan D., ed. 1988. *Rethinking History and Myth. Indigenous*

South American Perspectives on the Past. Champaign: University of Illinois Press.

Hinton, William. 1966. *Fanshen: A Documentary of Revolution in a Chinese Village*. New York: Vintage.

———. 1983. *Shenfan: The Continuing Revolution in a Chinese Village*. New York: Random House.

Hobsbawm, Eric, & Terence Ranger, eds. 1984. *The Invention of Tradition*. Cambridge, Eng.: Cambridge University Press.

Hsiao, Kung-chuan. 1960. *Rural China: Imperial Control in the Nineteenth Century*. Seattle: University of Washington Press.

Hu, Hsien-chin. 1948. *The Common Descent Group in China and Its Functions*. New York: Viking Fund Publications in Anthropology, no. 10.

Huang Chin-shing. 1993. "Power and Symbol: The Formation of the Confucius Temple's Ritual System" (Kongmiao jisi zhidu de xingcheng). *Dalu Zazhi* (Taibei: Academia Sinica), 86(5): 1–27.

Huang, Shu-min. 1989. *The Spiral Road: Change in a Chinese Village through the Eyes of a Communist Party Leader*. Boulder, Col.: Westview Press.

Hunt, Lynn. 1984. *Politics, Culture, and Class in the French Revolution*. Berkeley: University of California Press.

Hymes, Robert. 1986. "Marriage, Descent Groups, and the Localist Strategy in Sung and Yuan Fu-chou." In *Kinship Organization in Late Imperial China 1000–1940*. Ed. Patricia Ebrey & James L. Watson. Berkeley: University of California Press.

Jing Jun. 1989. "A Sociological Perspective on Relocation Projects for Reservoir Construction" (Shehuixue shiye nei de shuiku yimin gongcheng). *Rural Economy and Society* (Nongcun jingji yu shehui). (Beijing: Chinese Academy of Social Sciences), 5(11): 41–47.

Johnson, Graham. 1993. "Family Strategies and Economic Transformation in Rural China: Some Evidence from the Pearl River Delta." In *Chinese Families in the Post-Mao Era*. Ed. Deborah Davis & Stevan Harrell. Berkeley: University of California Press.

Jordan, David, & Daniel Overmyer. 1986. *The Flying Phoenix: Aspects of Chinese Sectarianism in Taiwan*. Princeton, N.J.: Princeton University Press.

Kane, Penny. 1988. *Famine in China, 1959–61: Demographic and Social Implications*. New York: St. Martin's Press.

Keesing, Roger. 1975. *Kinship Groups and Social Structure*. New York: Holt, Rinehart.

Kelliher, Daniel. 1992. *Peasant Power in China*. New Haven, Conn.: Yale University Press.

Kleinman, Arthur. 1986. *Social Origins of Distress and Disease*. New Haven, Conn.: Yale University Press.

———. 1991. "Suffering and Its Professional Transformation: Towards an Ethnography of Interpersonal Experience." *Culture, Medicine, and Psychiatry*, 15:275–301.

———. 1994. "How Bodies Remember: Social Memory and Bodily Experience of Criticism, Resistance, and Delegitimization Following China's Cultural Revolution. *New Literary History*, 25 (Summer): 707–23.

Kong Decheng. 1937. *Genealogy of the Confucius Family Clan (Kongzi shijia pu)*. Available at Harvard Yenching Library.

Kong Demao. 1984. *In the Mansion of Confucius: An Oral History*. Beijing: New World Press.

Kong Fanyin. 1992. *The Mansion of the Yansheng Dukes: An Eyewitness Account (Yansheng gongfu jianwen)*. Jinan: Qilu Press.

Kong Qinghui. 1948. *My Trip to Qufu to Get the Clan Genealogy (Qufu lingpu jixing)*. Available at Yongjing County Archives.

Kong Shangren. 1685. *Genealogy of the Confucius Family Clan (Kongzi shijia pu)*. Available at Harvard Yenching Library.

Kong Xiangguo. 1991. "Rites of Sacrificial Offering to Our Holy Ancestor" (Ji shengzu yishi). Manuscript.

Kong Xianmin. 1905. *Genealogy of the Kongs in Jincheng (Jincheng kongshi zupu)*. Available at Yongjing County Archives.

Kong Zhaozeng. 1934. *Qufu County Gazetteer (Qufu xianzhi)*. Available at Harvard Yenching Library.

Kuhn, Philip. 1970. *Rebellion and Its Enemies in Late Imperial China*. Cambridge, Mass.: Harvard University Press.

Kuper, Adam. 1983. "Les Femmes contre les boeufs." *L'Homme*, 27:33–54.

Lane, Christel. 1981. *The Rites of Rulers: Ritual in an Industrial Society—The Soviet Case*. Cambridge, Eng.: Cambridge University Press.

Langer, Lawrence. 1991. *Holocaust Testimonies: The Ruins of Memory*. New Haven, Conn.: Yale University Press.

Leach, Edmund. 1966. "Ritualization in Man in Relation to Conceptual and Social Development." *Philosophical Transactions of the Royal Society of London*, Series B, 251(722):403–8.

Lee, Thomas. 1985. *Government Education and Examinations in Sung China*. New York: St. Martin's.

Li Shengxian. 1990. "Farewell to the Chair-Shaped Tombs" (Biele yizi fen). *Tianjin Daily (Tianjin ribao)*. Aug. 26, p. 6.

Lieberthal, Kenneth. 1973. "The Suppression of Secret Societies in Post-Liberation Tientsin." *The China Quarterly*, 54:42–66.

Lindstrom, Lamont. 1982. "Leftamap Kastom: The Political History of Tradition on Tanna, Vanuatu." *Mankind*, 13: 316–29.

Linxia Prefectural Government. 1987. "An Outline of Our Proposal for Sharing Profits with the Three Hydrostations Built by the State in Linxia Prefecture and for Satisfactorily Solving the Problems of Living and Production among the Resettled Villagers" (Guanyu guojia jianzai linxiazhou jingnei sanzuo shuidianzhan gei difang rangli he tuoshan anzhi yimin shengchang shenghuo wenti de huibao tigang). Linxia, Gansu province.

Lipman, Jonathan. 1980. "The Border World of Gansu, 1895–1935." Ph.D. diss., Stanford University.

———. 1984. "Ethnicity and Politics in Republican China: The Ma Family Warlords of Gansu." *Modern China*, 10(3): 285–316.

———. 1990. "Ethnic Violence in Modern China: Hans and Huis in Gansu, 1781–1929." In *Violence in China*. Ed. Jonathan Lipman & Stevan Harrell. Albany: State University of New York Press.

Liu, Hui-chen. 1959. "An Analysis of Chinese Clan Rules: Confucian Theories in Action." In *Confucianism in Action*. Ed. David S. Nivison & Arthur F. Wright. Stanford, Calif.: Stanford University Press.

Liu Liming. 1993. *Ancestral Halls, Spirit Tablets, and Family Genealogies* (*Citang lingpai jiapu*). Chengdu: Sichuan People's Press.

Liu Youping. 1991. *Encyclopedia of Chinese Names: The Surname Wu* (*Zhongguo xing shi tong shu—wu xing*). Changsha: Sanhuan Press.

Lu Tianhong. 1988. *Certain Questions on the Compilation of Chinese City Gazetteers* (*Zhongguo chengshi zhi bianji de ruogan wenti*). Beijing: Yanshan Press.

Luo Wenhua & Nien Xinsen. 1991. *Encyclopedia of Chinese Names: The Surname Luo* (*Zhongguo xingshi tongshu: luo xing*). Changsha: Sanhuan Press.

MacFarquhar, Roderick. 1990. "The Succession to Mao and the End of Maoism." In *Cambridge History of China*, vol. 15. Ed. Roderick MacFarquhar & John King Fairbank. Cambridge, Eng.: Cambridge University Press.

MacInnis, Donald. 1989. *Religion in China Today: Policy and Practice*. Maryknoll, N.Y.: Orbis Books.

Mackerras, Colin. 1990. *Chinese Drama: A Historical Survey*. Beijing: New World Press.

Madsen, Richard. 1984. *Morality and Power in a Chinese Village*. Berkeley: University of California Press.

———. 1990. "The Politics of Revenge during the Cultural Revolution." In *Violence in China*. Ed. Jonathan Lipman & Stevan Harrell. Albany: State University of New York Press.

Mair, Victor. 1985. "Language and Ideology in the Popularizations of the Sacred Edicts." In *Popular Culture in Late Imperial China*. Ed. David Johnson, Andrew Nathan, & Evelyn Rawski. Berkeley: University of California Press.

Malinowski, Bronislaw. 1935. *Coral Gardens and Their Magic*. London: Allen & Unwin.

Meng Juxin. 1990. *The First Family under Heaven (Tianxia diyi jia)*. Jinan: Shandong Friendship Press.

Meskill, Johanna. 1970. "The Chinese Genealogy as a Research Source." In *Family and Kinship in Chinese Society*. Ed. Maurice Freedman. Stanford, Calif.: Stanford University Press.

Metzger, Thomas. 1977. *Neo-Confucianism and China's Evolving Culture*. New York: Columbia University Press.

Mintz, Alan. 1984. *Hurban: Response to Catastrophe in Hebrew Literature*. New York: Columbia University Press.

Miyazaki, Ichisada. 1976. *China's Examination Hell: The Civil Service Examinations of Imperial China*. Trans. Conrad Schirokaoer. New York: Weatherhill.

Moore, Sally F. 1986. *Social Facts and Fabrications: Customary Law on Kilimanjaro, 1880–1980*. Cambridge, Eng.: Cambridge University Press.

——. 1987. "Explaining the Present." *American Ethnologist*, 14(4): 727–36.

Moore, Sally F., & Barbara G. Meyerhoff, eds. 1977. *Secular Ritual: A Working Definition of Ritual*. Amsterdam: Van Gorcum.

Munn, Nancy. 1973. "Symbolism in Ritual Context: Aspects of Symbolic Action." In *Handbook of Social and Cultural Anthropology*. Ed. John Hongigmann. Chicago: Rand McNally.

Naquin, Susan. 1976. *Millenarian Rebellion in China: The Eight Trigrams Uprising in 1813*. New Haven, Conn.: Yale University Press.

Neisser, Ulric. 1978. "Memory: What Are the Important Questions?" In *Practical Aspects of Memory*. Ed. M. M. Gruneberg, P. E. Morris, & R. N. Sykes. London: Academic Press.

——. 1982. "Snapshots or Benchmarks?" In *Memory Observed: Remembering in Natural Context*. Ed. Ulric Neisser. San Francisco: W. H. Freeman.

Nivison, David S., & Arthur F. Wright, eds. 1959. *Confucianism in Action*. Stanford, Calif.: Stanford University Press.

Ong, Walter. 1977. *Interfaces of the Word*. Ithaca, N.Y.: Cornell University Press.

——. [1982] 1988. *Orality and Literacy*. London: Routledge.

Ouyang Fa & Ding Jian. 1986. *Twelve Lectures on Compiling New Local Gazetteers (Xinbian fangzhi shi'er jiang)*. Hefei: Huangshan Press.

Pasternak, Burton. 1972. *Kinship and Community in Two Chinese Villages*. Stanford, Calif.: Stanford University Press.

People's Education Press. [1988] 1991. *A Primary School Textbook: Chinese Language Lessons (Xiaoxue keben: yuwen)*. Beijing.

Perry, Elizabeth J. 1980. *Rebels and Revolutionaries in North China, 1845–1945*. Stanford, Calif.: Stanford University Press.

———. 1983. "Social Banditry Revisited." *Modern China*, 9(3): 355–82.

Popular Memory Group. 1982. "Popular Memory, Theory and Method." In *Making Histories: Studies in History-writing and Politics*. Ed. Richard Johnson, Gregory McLennan, Bill Schwarz, & David Sutton. Minneapolis: University of Minnesota Press.

Potter, Jack M. 1970. *Land and Lineage in Traditional China*. In *Confucianism in Action*. Ed. David S. Nivison & Arthur F. Wright. Stanford, Calif.: Stanford University Press.

Potter, Jack M., & Sulamith Heins Potter. 1990. *China's Peasants: The Anthropology of a Revolution*. Cambridge, Eng.: Cambridge University Press.

Qi Wu. 1982. *The Manor of the Kong Landlords (Kongshi dizhu zhuangyuan)*. Beijing: Chinese Academy of Social Sciences Press.

Rambo, Karl. 1990. "Jesus Came Here Too: The Making of a Cultural Hero and Control over History in Simbu, Papua New Guinea." *Ethnology*, 29: 177–87.

Rappaport, Joanne. 1990. *The Politics of Memory: Native Historical Interpretation in the Colombian Andes*. Cambridge, Eng.: Cambridge University Press.

Rawski, Evelyn. 1979. *Education and Popular Literacy in Ch'ing China*. Ann Arbor: University of Michigan Press.

Reber, Arthur. 1985. *Dictionary of Psychology*. New York: Penguin.

Rosaldo, Renato. 1980. *Ilongot Headhunting, 1883–1974: A Study in Society and History*. Stanford, Calif.: Stanford University Press.

Ruf, Gregory. 1994. "Pillars of the State: Laboring Families, Authority, and Community in Rural Sichuan, 1937–1991." Ph.D. diss., Columbia University.

Ryckmans, Pierre (Simon Leys). 1986. *The Chinese Attitude Towards the Past*. Canberra: 47th George Morrison Lecture in Ethnology.

Sahlins, Marshall. 1972. *Stone Age Economics*. New York: Aldine De Gruyter.

Sampson, Geoffrey. 1985. *Writing Systems*. Stanford, Calif.: Stanford University Press.

Sangren, Steven. 1987. *History and Magical Power in a Chinese Com-munity.* Stanford, Calif.: Stanford University Press.

Schuman, Howard, & Jacqueline Scott. 1989. "Generations and Collec-tive Memory." *American Sociological Review,* 54: 359–81.

Schwarcz, Vera. 1987. "Out of Historical Amnesia." *Modern China,* 13(2): 177–225.

———. 1991. "No Solace from Lethe: History, Memory, and Cultural Identity in Twentieth-Century China." *Daedalus,* 120(1): 85–109. Reprinted in Tu Wei-ming, ed. *The Living Tree: The Changing Mean-ing of Being Chinese Today.* Stanford, Calif.: Stanford University Press [1994].

———. 1994. "Strangers No More: Personal Memory in the Interstices of Public Commemoration." In *Memory, History, and Opposition.* Ed. Rubie Watson. Santa Fe, N.M.: School of American Research Press.

Schwartz, Barry. 1982. "The Social Context of Commemoration: A Study in Collective Memory." *Social Forces,* 61(2): 374–97.

———. 1991. "Social Change and Collective Memory: The Democrati-zation of George Washington." *American Sociological Review,* 56 (April: 221–36).

Scott, James C. 1985. *Weapons of the Weak: Everyday Forms of Peasant Resistance.* New Haven, Conn.: Yale University Press.

Scudder, Thayer. 1973. "The Human Ecology of Big Projects: River Ba-sin Development and Resettlement." *Annual Review of Anthropol-ogy,* pp. 45–55.

Shen Qixin. 1991. *Encyclopedia of Chinese Names: The Surname Zhao (Zhongguo xingshi tongshu—zhao xing).* Changsha: Sanhuan Press.

Shi Deng. 1871. *Panyu County Gazetteer (Panyu xianzhi).* Available at Harvard Yenching Library.

———. 1879. *Guangzhou Prefecture Gazetteer (Guangzhou fuzhi).* Available at Harvard Yenching Library.

Shirk, Susan. 1982. *Competitive Comrades: Career Incentives and Stu-dent Strategies in China.* Berkeley: University of California Press.

Shkilnyk, Anastasia. 1985. *Poison Stronger Than Love.* New Haven, Conn.: Yale University Press.

Shryock, John. [1932] 1966. *The Origin and Development of the State Cult of Confucius.* New York: Paragon.

Shue, Vivienne. 1980. *Peasant China in Transition: The Dynamics of Development Towards Socialism, 1949–1956.* Berkeley: University of California Press.

Sima Qian. 1972. *Records of the Grand Historian (Shi ji).* Beijing: Zhonghua Books.

Siu, Helen F. 1989a. *Agents and Victims in South China: Accomplices in Rural Revolution*. New Haven, Conn.: Yale University Press.

———. 1989b. "Socialist Peddlers and Princes in a Chinese Market Town." *American Ethnologist*, 16(2): 195–212.

———. 1990. "Recycling Tradition: Culture, History, and Political Economy in the Chrysanthemum Festivals of South China." *Comparative Study of Society and History*, 32(4): 765–94.

Siu, Helen F., & Zelda Stern. 1983. *Mao's Harvest: Voices from China's New Generation*. New York: Oxford University Press.

Smil, Vaclav. 1984. *The Bad Earth: Environmental Degradation in China*. Armonk, N.Y.: M. E. Sharpe.

———. 1993. *China's Environmental Crisis: An Inquiry into the Limits of National Development*. Armonk, N.Y.: M. E. Sharpe.

Smith, Robertson. [1889] 1956. *The Religion of the Semites*. New York: Meridian.

Spence, Jonathan. 1990. *The Search for Modern China*. New York: Norton.

State Statistics Bureau. 1992. *Statistical Yearbook of China*. Beijing: China Statistics Press.

———. 1993a. *Monthly Review of Prices and Incomes in China*.

———. 1993b. *Statistical Yearbook of China*.

Sun Jian, ed. 1982. *Selected Archives of the Kong Mansion (Kongfu tang'an xuanbian)*. Beijing: Zhonghua Books.

Taga, Akigoro. 1960. *An Analytical Study of Chinese Genealogical Books (Sofu no kenkyu)*. Tokyo: Toyo Bunko.

Tambiah, Stanley. 1985. *Culture, Thought, and Social Action*. Cambridge, Mass.: Harvard University Press.

Tanaka, Issei. 1981. *A Study of Ritual Theaters in China (Chugoku saishhi engeki kenkyu)*. Tokyo: Toyo Cultural Research Institute.

———. 1985. "The Social and Historical Context of Ming-Ch'ing Local Drama." In *Popular Culture in Late Imperial China*. Ed. David Johnson, Andrew Nathan, & Evelyn Rawski. Berkeley: University of California Press.

Taylor, Rodney. 1990. *The Religious Dimensions of Confucianism*. Albany: State University of New York Press.

Teng, Ssu-yu, & John King Fairbank, eds. 1963. *China's Response to the West: A Documentary Survey, 1839–1923*. New York: Atheneum.

Tian Fan & Lin Fatang. 1986. *Population Movements in China (Zhongguo renkou qianyi)*. Beijing: Zhishi Press.

Tianjin Municipal Party Committee. 1991. *Eradicating Superstitious Beliefs in Ghosts and Deities (Pochu guishen mixin)*. Tianjin: Tianjin Academy of Social Sciences Press.

Tu, Weiming. 1979. "Shifting Perspectives on Text and History: A Reflection on Shelly Errington's Paper." *Journal of Asian Studies*, 38: 245–51.

Tuan, Yi-fu. 1977. *Space and Place*. Minneapolis: University of Minnesota Press.

Turner, Victor. 1961. "Ritual Symbolism, Morality, and Social Structure among the Ndembu." *Rhodes Livingstone Journal*. No. 30. Manchester: Manchester University Press.

———. 1962. "Three Symbols of Passage in Ndembu Circumcision Ritual." In *Essays on the Ritual of Social Relations*. Ed. Max Gluckman. Manchester: Manchester University Press.

———. 1969. *Ritual Process*. Chicago: Aldine.

———. 1974. *Dramas, Fields, and Metaphors*. Ithaca, N.Y.: Cornell University Press.

Unger, Jonathan, ed. 1993. *Using the Past to Serve the Present: Historiography and Politics in Contemporary China*. Armonk, N.Y.: M. E. Sharpe.

Valensi, Lucette. 1986. "From Sacred History to Historical Memory and Back: The Jewish Past." *History and Anthropology*, 2(2): 283–305.

van Gennep, Arnold. [1909] 1960. *The Rites of Passage*. Chicago: University of Chicago Press.

Vansina, Jan. 1985. *Oral Tradition as History*. Madison: University of Wisconsin Press.

Vogel, Ezra. 1969. "Land Reform in Kwangtung, 1951–53: Central Control and Localism." *The China Quarterly*, 38: 27–62.

Wakeman, Frederic E. 1972. "The Secret Societies in Kwangtung, 1800–1856." In *Popular Movements and Secret Societies in China: 1840–1950*. Ed. Jean Chesneaux. Stanford, Calif.: Stanford University Press.

Wang Bin. 1989. "How Should Funerary Customs Be Reformed in the Countryside?" (Nongcun binzang yinggai zenyang gao). *China Peasant News* (*Zhongguo nongmin bao*), May 3, p. 4.

Wang Huning, ed. 1991. *Villages, Family Groups, and Culture in Contemporary China* (*Tangdai zhongguo cunluo jiazu wenhua*). Shanghai: Shanghai People's Press.

Wang Weimin. 1989. "A Study of Reservoir Resettlement on the Upper Reaches of the Yellow River" (Huanghe shanyou shuiku yimin yanjiu) (manuscript). Beijing University: Institute of Sociology.

Watson, James L. 1975. *Emigration and the Chinese Lineage*. Berkeley: University of California Press.

———. 1982a. "Of Flesh and Bones: The Management of Death Pollution in Cantonese Society." In *Death and the Regeneration of Life*.

Ed. Maurice Bloch & Jonathan Parry. Cambridge, Eng.: Cambridge University Press.

———. 1982b. "Chinese Kinship Reconsidered: Anthropological Analysis of Historical Research." *The China Quarterly*, 92: 589–622.

———. 1985. "Standardizing the Gods: The Promotion of T'ien Hou Along the South China Coast, 960–1960." In *Popular Culture in Late Imperial China*. Ed. David Johnson, Andrew Nathan, & Evelyn Rawski. Berkeley: University of California Press.

———. 1986. "Anthropological Overview: The Development of Chinese Descent Groups." In *Kinship Organization in Late Imperial China, 1000–1940*. Ed. Patricia Ebrey & James L. Watson. Berkeley: University of California Press.

———. 1987. "From the Common Pot: Feasting with Equals in Chinese Society." *Anthropos*, 82: 389–401.

———. 1988. "Funeral Specialists in Cantonese Society." In *Death Rituals in Late Imperial and Modern China*. Ed. James L. Watson and Evelyn S. Rawski. Berkeley: University of California Press.

Watson, Rubie. 1985. *Inequality Among Brothers: Class and Kinship in South China*. Cambridge, Eng.: Cambridge University Press.

———. 1988. "Remembering the Dead: Graves and Politics in Southeastern China." In *Death Rituals in Late Imperial and Modern China*. Ed. James L. Watson & Evelyn S. Rawski. Berkeley: University of California Press.

———. 1994. "Making Secret Histories: Memory and Mourning in Post-Mao China." In *Memory, History, and Opposition Under State Socialism*. Ed. Rubie Watson. Santa Fe, N.M.: School of American Research.

Watters, Thomas. 1879. *A Guide to the Tablets in a Temple of Confucius*. Shanghai: Presbyterian Mission Press.

Wei Hanwen. 1988. *A Profile of Prefectures and Counties in Gansu (Gansu dixian gaikuang)*. Lanzhou: Gansu Statistics Bureau.

Welch, Holmes. 1965. *Taoism: The Parting of the Way*. Boston: Beacon Press.

Weller, Robert. 1987. *Unities and Diversities in Chinese Religion*. Seattle: University of Washington Press.

Wilson, Thomas A. 1995a. *Genealogy of the Way: The Construction and Uses of the Confucian Tradition in Later Imperial China*. Stanford, Calif.: Stanford University Press.

———. 1995b. "The Ritualization of Confucian Orthodoxy and the Descendants of the Sage." Paper presented to the Neo-Confucian Seminar, Columbia University.

Winograd, Eugene, & William Killinger. 1983. "Relating Age at Encoding in Early Childhood to Adult Recall: Development of Flash-bulb Memories." *Journal of Experimental Psychology: General*, 112:413–22.

Wolf, Arthur P. 1970. "Chinese Kinship and Mourning Dress." In *Family and Kinship in Chinese Society*. Ed. Maurice Freedman. Stanford, Calif.: Stanford University Press.

World Bank. 1988. *China: Growth and Development in Gansu Province*. Washington, D.C.

Wright, Arthur F. 1960. *The Confucian Persuasion*. Stanford, Calif.: Stanford University Press.

Xue Jialu, ed. 1991. *Dictionary of Ritual Customs in Ancient China (Zhongguo gudai lisu cidian)*. Beijing: Friendship Press.

Ya Zi & Liang Zi. 1992. *Qufu's Big Disaster (Qufu dajienan)*. Hong Kong: Tianditushu (Cosmos Books).

Yan, Yunxiang. 1992. "The Impact of Reform on Economic and Social Stratification in a Chinese Village." *Australian Journal of Chinese Affairs*, 27:1–23.

———. 1993. "The Flow of Gifts: Reciprocity and Social Networks in a Chinese Village." Ph.D. diss., Harvard University.

Yang, C. K. 1959. *Chinese Communist Society: The Family and the Village*. Cambridge, Mass.: MIT Press.

———. 1961. *Religion in Chinese Society*. Berkeley: University of California Press.

Yang, Mayfair. 1986. *Gifts, Favors, and Banquets: The Art of Social Relationships and Exchange in China*. Ithaca, N.Y.: Cornell University Press.

———. 1989. "The Gift Economy and State Power in China." *Comparative Studies in Society and History*, 31(1):25–54.

———. 1993. "Tradition, Travelling Anthropology, and the Discourse of Modernity in China." Paper presented at the Fourth Decennial Conference of the Association of Social Anthropology, Oxford University. Forthcoming in *What Is Anthropological Knowledge For?* Ed. Henrietta Moore. New York: Routledge.

Yang Weimin. 1989. "Thousands of Tombs Appeared at Baiyunshan" (Baiyunshan maochu qianjia zhong). *People's Daily (Renmin ribao)*, Aug. 27, p. 8.

Yates, Frances. 1966. *The Art of Memory*. Chicago: University of Chicago Press.

Yongjing County Gazetteer Committee. 1992. *Yongjing County Gazetteer (Yongjing xianzhi)*.

Yongjing County Government. 1987. "A Report on the Existing Problems of Reservoir Resettlement in Yongjing County" (Yongjingxian yimin qianyi qingkuang ji cunzai wenti de baokao).

Yun, Cai. 1988. "Don't Forget Eliminating Ignorance along with Poverty" (Zhiqiong mowang zhiyu). *Chinese Culture Newspaper* (*Zhongguo wenhu bao*), Mar. 16, p. 2.

Zhang Chi & Jin Shi. 1991. *Illustrated Biographies of Confucius's Seventy-Two Disciples* (*Kongzi qishi er dizi tupu*). Beijing: China Peace Press.

Zhang Guochang. [1892] 1917. *Revised Gazetteer of Gaolan County* (*Chongxiu gaolan xianzhi*). Available at Gansu Provincial Library.

Zhang Weihua, ed. 1980. *Selected Historical Material from the Archives of Qufu's Kong Mansion* (*Qufu kongfu tang'an shiliao xuanbian*). Jinan: Qilu Press.

Zhang Xiumin. [1962] 1990. "Wooden Movable Printing Boards in the Qing Dynasty" (Qingdai de muhuozi). In *The Origin and Development of Movable Printing Boards* (*Huozi yinshua yuanliu*). Ed. Zhang Shudong. Beijing: Printing Industry Press.

Zhang Yue. 1988. "Migration and Development" (Yimin yu fazhan). *Forum on Rural Issues* (*Nongcun wenti luntan*). Document No. 138. Beijing: Research Center for Rural Development, State Council.

Zhang Zhongying. 1989. *An Exploratory Study in the Art of Writing Contemporary Gazetteers* (*Tangdai fangzhixue tanlun*). Chengdu: Bashu Press.

Zhao Wenlin & Xie Shujun. 1988. *A Demographic History of China* (*Zhongguo renkou shi*). Beijing: Beijing People's Press.

Zonabend, Françoise. 1985. *The Enduring Memory: Time and History in a French Village.* Manchester: Manchester University Press.

Character List

bai hua　白话
bai ta si　白塔寺
bao jia　保甲
bao zhang　保长
cai hong qiao　彩虹桥
cha hua　插花
chang qing guan　常青观
cheng fen　成份
chu shen　出身
chun fen　春分
ci　祠
ci tang　祠堂
cun gan bu　村干部
da cheng dian　大成殿
da dao hui　大刀会
da jia zhang　大家长
da ming　大名
da yuan zhu　大愿主
da zong hu　大宗户
dai li de　带礼的
dai shi ping　代食品
dao de hui　道德会
di fan zhi　地方志
dui lian　对联
er hu　二胡

er yuan zhu　二愿主
fan dong hui dao men
　反动会道门
fan ti zi　繁体字
fang shen miao　方神庙
fen guan　分管
fu zi dong　夫子洞
ga miao　尕庙
gan hui de　赶会的
gang lie　刚烈
gong de lin　功德林
gong fen　工分
guan　观
guo ji　国祭
guo nian　过年
han yin　翰音
hang dao lao zhe　巷道老者
hou　候
hou kao　后靠
hu　户
huai fen zi　坏份子
huang li　皇历
hui hui tai　回回台
ji tian　祭田
ji wen　祭文

205

jia fa   家法
jian ti zi   简体字
jin cheng   金城
jin hua miao   金花庙
jing ben   经本
ju shi   居士
kong fu zi   孔夫子
kong meng hui   孔孟会
kong miao   孔庙
kong shi jia zu   孔氏家族
kong zi miao   孔子庙
kong zi shi ji pu   孔子世家谱
lao jiao   老教
lao pu zi   老堡子
lao shu ji   老书记
lao zhuang   老庄
li sheng   礼生
liang xin dao   良心道
ling nan pai   岭南派
ling pai   灵牌
liu shi zong hu   六十宗户
liu yu hu   流寓户
lun yu   论语
luo jia dong   罗家洞
luo pan   罗盘
miao   庙
ming qian   命签
ming shi   明视
nei jiu   内疚
nei yuan kong   内院孔
pin xie   贫协
pu guan   谱馆
pu tong qun zhong   普通群众
qin qiang   秦腔
qing cha deng ji   清察登记
qing ming   清明
rou mao   柔毛
shan shu   善书
shang hang dao   上巷道
shang xiang   尚飨
shen han   神汉
shen wei   神位

sheng ji tu   圣跡图
sheng ren   圣人
sheng ren dian   圣人殿
sheng zu   圣祖
shi da fu   士大夫
shi ji   史记
shi xi tu   世系图
shu zui   赎罪
si   寺
si lei fen zi   四类份子
si men   四门
song shen   送神
wa fang   瓦房
wai yuan kong   外院孔
wei kong   伪孔
wen miao   文庙
wen xian hu   文献户
wen yan   文言
wu fu   五服
wu po   巫婆
wu zhuang bu   武装部
xia tiao zi de   下条子的
xian li   献礼
xian sheng miao   先圣庙
xiang qi   象棋
xiao ming   小名
xiao zong hu   小宗户
xin fang zhi   新方志
xin si   新寺
xing ru sheng shi   兴儒盛世
yan jia wan   颜家湾
yan sheng gong   衍圣公
yang zhai   阳宅
yin yang   阴阳
yin zhai   阴宅
ying sheng jia li   迎圣驾礼
ying sheng li   迎牲礼
yuan zhu   愿主
zhong xing zu   中兴祖
zhu rou   猪肉
zu ting   族庭
zu zhang   族长

Index

In this index an "f" after a number indicates a separate reference on the next page, and an "ff" indicates separate references on the next two pages. A continuous discussion over two or more pages is indicated by a span of page numbers, e.g., "57–59." *Passim* is used for a cluster of references in close but not consecutive sequence.

Agnatic kinship, *see* Kinship structure
Ancestor charts (*shen zhu*), 138, 182n4, 182–83n6. *See also* Spirit tablets
Ancestor halls, 23, 65, 147
Ancestor worship: post-Mao resumption of, 28–29, 89–90, 102; spirit tablet arrangement and, 28–29, 58–59, 65–66; state sponsorship of, 33–34, 125–26, 127; sacrificial rites of, 103–4; ceremonial occasions of, 123–25, 182nn3–4; ancestor charts in, 138, 182–83nn5–6; as public event, 145, 148–51, 175–76, 185n8; rules of avoidance in, 146–48; opera performances and, 158–60, 183–84n3. *See also* Confucius; Genealogies; Temple festival

Ancestral Line Restorer (*zhong xing zu*), 35
Ancestral remains, *see* Tombs
The Ancient City: A Study on the Religion, Laws, and Institutions of Greece and Rome (*La cité antique*, Foustel de Coulanges), 144
Ancient Saint Temples (*xian sheng miao*), 24
Anthropology: memory research in, 13–17; genealogical controversy in, 116, 181n1
Anti–Feudal Privilege Campaign, 51–52
Anti–Lin Biao and Confucius Campaign, *see* Campaign Against Lin Biao and Confucius
Anti-superstition handbook, 174–75, 184–85n6
Appadurai, Arjun, 89

Tian Fan and Lin Fatang, 184n1
Tombs, 2, 79–85 passim, 143,
   179n3, 180nn3–4
Tongzhi Emperor (1862–74), 24
La Topographie légendaire des évangiles en terre saint: Etude de
   mémoire collective (Halbwachs),
   15, 178n7
Township officials, see Village
   cadres
Turner, Victor, 144

Unit commander (fen guan), 48

Valensi, Lucette, 164–65
Van Gennep, Arnold, 106, 144
Vernacular language (bai hua), 108
Village cadres (cun gan bu): commune role of, 9–10; decollectivization impact on, 11, 18–19,
   178n6; as state collaborators, 19,
   87, 89, 137–38; resettlement
   responsibility of, 75, 179–80n2;
   ritual authority of, 89–90; government's replacement of, 93–
   96, 102; new generation of, 98–
   99, 180n2; revenge against, 167–
   68
Village chief accountant, 120, 140
Village chief administrator, 7
Village informants, 7, 119–20, 140;
   memories of, 55–57, 74–83 passim; guilt feelings of, 79–80, 84–
   85
Vow-takers (yuan zhu), see Temple
   managers

Wang Bing, 184n4
Watson, James, 81, 119, 122, 125–
   26
Watson, Rubie, 169
Wei dynasty, 34
Wen Di, Emperor, 34
Wen Tianxiang, 133
Wen yan (classical Chinese), 107–
   8, 110. See also Ritual language

Wenzhou, 174
White Pagoda Monastery (bai ta
   si), 185n8
Women: ritual guidelines for, 66f,
   147–55 passim
Work points (gong fen), 9
World Bank, 184n2
Written text: on ritual objects, 83,
   85–86, 138f, 180n4, 182n5; in
   wen yan, 107–8; simplified vs.
   traditional, 108–14 passim,
   181n2; mnemonic implications
   of, 111–13; governmental reform
   of, 113–14, 181n4; sacred quality
   of, 140, 183n7. See also
   Genealogies
Wu Di, Emperor, 31

Xian, 5
Xiaochuan, 41, 130, 132, 145, 151
Xiaochuan genealogy, see Kong
   clan genealogy (1905)
Xia River, 71
Xinjiang, 3, 5

Yang, Mayfair, 174
Yanguoxia Hydropower Station,
   69–77 passim, 92, 166, 177n1
Yangzi River region, 118
Yan Hui, 57
Yanjiawan (Yan family terrace), 58,
   123, 132
Yansheng dukes, 30, 36–39, 65. See
   also Kongs of Qufu
Yan Yunxiang, 19
Yates, Frances, 171–72
Yellow River: dam projects on, 1,
   43–44, 71–72, 75–76, 127, 177n1
Yenching Library, Harvard University, 42, 119
Yongjing county, 7; Kongs' presence in, 43–44, 131–32, 179n2;
   secret societies of, 47; antireligious campaigns in, 51–52, 54–
   55; hydraulic projects in, 71–74,
   179n1; decollectivization in, 90–

Library of Congress Cataloging-in-Publication Data

Jing, Jun, 1957–
    The temple of memories : history, power, and morality in a Chinese
village / Jun Jing.
        p.   cm.
    Includes bibliographical references and index.
    ISBN 0-8047-2756-2 (alk. paper)
    1. Kansu Province (China)–Social conditions.   2. K'ung family.
3. Memory–Social aspects–China–Kansu Province.   I. Title.
HN740.K365J56   1996
306'.095145–dc20   96-15406
                                                                                        CIP

⊗ This book is printed on acid–free paper
Original printing 1996
Last figure below indicates year of this printing
05   04   03   02   01   00